The Secret to
Winning the Corporate Game

Rodney S. Jones

PAGE PUBLISHING, INC.
Conneaut Lake, PA

First originally published by Page Publishing 2020

ISBN 978-1-6624-0605-8 (pbk)
ISBN 978-1-6624-1900-3 (hc)
ISBN 978-1-6624-0606-5 (digital)

Printed in the United States of America

THE PLAYBOOK

PRE-GAME SPEECH

FIRST HALF GAME PLAN

SECOND HALF GAME PLAN

Foreword

· ·

I must admit, when I was asked to write the foreword to his debut book, I was, to say the least, intimidated. With such a daunting task, would I be able to do the book and him justice?

Then I thought, *I'm his wife. Who else is better suited to give you a glimpse of the man I've known for over half of my life?*

On social media, he goes by @iteachcharisma. His fraternity brothers know him as Nat King Cold. On stage, when he's addressing an audience, he's Mr. Corporate Swagger. To me, he's Rodney—my other half. I hope to give you the reader just a small snapshot of the man behind the titles.

I first met Rodney in the eighth grade at a rival school's basketball game. He was shy and soft-spoken. He happened to be a mutual friend of my best friend. Although he doesn't remember our first meeting, in that moment, he had already made an impression on me. Later that year we would become the best of friends and each other's secret crush. He was my confidant, the one I'd run to when I had the typical teenage drama-queen meltdowns with my boyfriend. We have different points of view or recollections of what happened next, but let's just say after a lot of miscommunications and misfires, our friendship ended. Ultimately, after graduation, we lost touch.

Fast forward several years—I started searching for Rodney on social media when I had gone through another drama-queen meltdown. I wanted to find someone to have solace and comfort in. I remembered that Rodney was that for me and wanted to reconnect to that calming feeling. I wanted to remember and regain a piece of myself that I had lost. Before he was inspiring audiences and delivering keynotes, he had an innate ability to make people feel bigger than they were. Even as a shy teenager, he had this way to help others see their true self-worth. I guess you could say I was his first coaching client. He was the key. During a chance meeting and conversation with a high school classmate I learned some valuable information to find him on Facebook some seventeen years after losing touch. While he was trying to impress me by parading his newfound bravado, I was laughing in his face. He may have replaced the shyness with confidence, but beneath it all was the same Rodney Jones from biology class that loved to make people feel good about themselves."

Over years of getting to know him as his friend, girlfriend, fiancé, and now wife, I have seen Rodney evolve into not only a great man but also one of the best humans I know. He's still the compassionate, kind, supportive kid I grew to love way back when, but now he has added layers. For me to convey all the admiration I have for him would take up most of these pages, so I'll just keep it to a collection of words and phrases that come to my mind:

- Big heart
- Charismatic
- Sincere
- Biggest cheerleader
- Tells you what only your closest BFF would tell you
- There with you every step of the way
- The thing, that magic, you can't put your finger on
- He's been there and struggled so you wouldn't have to
- Underdog
- Champion
- To him there's no such thing as "can't" or "not being good enough"
- Wants you to win that unwinnable fight
- Sees the greatness within that no one else sees
- Like Emeril Lagasse—when a recipe is missing something then BAM!
- The best thing you never knew you needed

So with all that being said, I know this book will be the perfect coaching tool you need to help you advance to that next level in your career and life. I've had the honor to watch from the sidelines and am excited to see success uncovered.

Humbly,
Enna P. Jones

Acknowledgments

God has put a passion in my heart to help people see the better version of themselves that may be buried underneath years of defeat, negativity, and unfulfilled dreams. He's the first person I have to acknowledge. I thank Him for seeing enough in me to entrust me with this assignment. One of my favorite scriptures is found in 1 Corinthians where Paul writes that God deliberately chose men and women that the culture overlooks and exploits and abuses, chose these "nobodies" to expose the hollow pretensions of the "somebodies." Thank you, God.

I have to thank the young lady at my first speaking engagement in 2010. I wish I knew her name. She was the one who met me at the bottom of the stage immediately after I had finished speaking. With gleeful anticipation, she asked if I had written a book on Corporate Swagger because she said she would love to read it. Unfortunately, I had to tell her no. Many thanks because it was her voice in my head for the last nine years that pushed me to finally complete this project.

To the sixteen people who so graciously set aside personal time to contribute their wisdom, I am exceedingly thankful: Summer McElroy, a beast on the Spartan course and a beast in the courtroom; Tyra Metoyer, a multifaceted specialist who gets stuff done; Steven Coleman, the epitome of going after a dream and teaching others how to do the same; Sarah Bolka, an icon for confidence in the face of battle; Joseph Norman, the consummate professional and the person you want in your corner when things go south; Darryl Blackburn, the quintessential example of business excellence and real talk; Charles Epps, the perfect combination of moxie and acumen;

9

Veronica Brooks, iron sharpens iron and her commitment to holding me accountable helped to keep me on schedule; Melinda "Mindy" Wisenbaker, a valuable ally in helping emerging professionals navigate the professional ranks; Alexandra McCauley, you're the intersection of competitive spirit and customer service, where excellence lives; Courtney Elveston, proof that faith has a place in business; Steven Linton, the Morpheus to my Neo—you taught me, pushed me, believed in me, and trusted me; Lesia Linton, you're the reason why minority women are to be taken seriously in the business world; Thoma Brewer, no team is complete without you—inside and out of the boardroom; Anthony Rosette, you're the total package when it comes to the qualities of a true leader; Byrena Washington, the holder of the golden scrolls to parlaying obscure beginnings into an executive position. All of you embody the essence of Corporate Swagger. Thank you for your gift.

My daughter, Daphne, you're the unassuming encouragement that I never imagined having. Every day I get to watch you blossom into the powerhouse you're destined to be. Thank you for loving me and letting me be your daddy. Never have I been around such positivity, optimism, joy, and sheer happiness of the likes of you. Quality time is your love language, and I know I took some of that away from you during this project. Through it all, you never made me feel bad and you never complained. I owe you. Thanks for letting me be your daddy.

Enna, I type these words with tears in my eyes. Who am I to deserve someone like you? I remember in 2010 when I told you I wanted to be a professional speaker, you laughed. For a split second I questioned if I should continue dating you. How could I be with someone who didn't believe in my dreams? Then days later, unexpectedly, I got a package in the mail. In it were three books on how to become a professional speaker. You told me that you laughed because you didn't think I was serious enough to do the work necessary to become a professional speaker. You were right because you did for me what I didn't think to do for myself: you invested in me. You've been investing in me ever since. You've invested belief, trust, motivation, inspiration, admiration, support, emotional stability, comfort, love, and so much more. The Bible says that he who finds a wife finds a good thing and favor from the Lord. Without you, there's no favor to take the stage for the first time and every time thereafter. Without you, I wouldn't have the confidence to coach others. Without you, these pages would not have gotten written. Behind it all, you were the voice telling me "You're valuable. People need what you have." Without you, I would have folded at the feet of the imposter syndrome. Because of you, and the grace of God, I am what I am. I love you and thank you.

Introduction

. . . .

Let me lay down some gratitude before I go any further. I sincerely thank you for expending the effort to choose this book and read this much of it. There are an infinite number of books you could be considering right now. I appreciate you for giving this one a shot. My hope is to keep you engaged for just a bit longer.

Second, let me save you a lot of time by helping you decide if this is for you or not. I want you to think about a time when you went after something with every fiber of your being. It could have been a job interview, a promotion, a major client, a chance to start your own business, or perhaps even a date with that special someone. On the surface, all advantages pointed in your favor. The tale of the tape leaned heavily in your direction from top to bottom. Technically and statistically, you were a lock. The optics painted the perfect picture that featured you as the ideal choice. Why not you, right? Yet after pouring everything you had into whatever it was you were going after, it wasn't enough. You didn't get the promotion. The client chose a different company. Your pitch fell flat. You were once again passed over for someone else. Game over, you lost. I'm telling you right now, stay woke! There *is* a game being played with rules that are sometimes unspoken. How can you win under those circumstances? How can you expect to have a chance if you don't have all the tools? If you can relate to coming up a hair short despite checking all the boxes, then consider what you have in your hand to be the other team's playbook.

If that scenario is foreign to you and you find yourself saying, "That ain't me," then you're probably either very lucky, very privileged, or haven't had enough life experiences to leave you feeling like you just had your lunch money taken. If you're lucky, it's only a matter of time before your luck runs out. Remember, the house always wins. Your time at the craps table will come to an end once the house starts asserting its position and your luck runs out. When that happens, then what? If you're privileged, imagine yourself in the selection process with other privileged people. There's only one person getting picked, and everyone rode in on a similar coattail. Once that happens, then what? Let's say you're young and lacking credit hours at the University of Life. You're definitely at a disadvantage. In case you didn't know, EQ > IQ all day. Your GPA and double major will get glossed over very easily when compared to someone with just as much knowledge as you *and* more real-world experience. Then what? At this point you'll either keep reading or walk away in denial. I'd like to take this opportunity to give a shout-out to one of my favorite rap groups, Goodie Mob. To you my friend, I offer up this lyric from their song "Cell Therapy," "Listen to me now…believe me later on." When it happens, you'll realize I wrote this with you in mind as well. They say people either learn by wisdom or experience. Trust me on this one. Take the wisdom route. You'll thank me later.

For those of you who find it easy to relate to the plights of someone who had to claw, scrape, and fight just to remain somewhat relevant in their field or workplace, then that proves that you've felt it. Remember that job interview? You prepared as if you were putting together a multimillion-dollar company acquisition brief. You knew which questions they were going to ask, and your answers were brilliant. You put on your favorite underwear because you wanted to summon every ounce of voodoo juju available. You knew the company inside and out. You got there an hour early because you were extra careful not to let something trivial like tardiness ruin your chances. This job was yours, and there was never a doubt. Then you heard the all-too-familiar words, "Thank you, but we're going to go in a different direction." Right there, you felt it.

Remember the school project? You worked on it for weeks. You sacrificed kicking it with your friends because you knew the reward would be much greater than getting somebody's number at a party only to find out they weren't really all that fine. I digress. Your research was undeniable. Your visuals were dripping with QLED 4K television quality. You even had James Earl Jones narrate it. For my younger readers, he's the voice of Darth Vader without the asthmatic reverb, the same cat that did the voice of Mufasa from *Lion King* (1994). Anyway, the day comes for you to give your presentation. You delivered what you thought was a good enough job to get an A. You got your grade back, and it's far lower than you expected. To make matters worse, you find out that your classmate who put in less time to prepare got a higher grade than you. Right there, you felt it.

Remember that client sales pitch? You had been professionally persistent to get this meeting. All you needed was fifteen minutes of their time. After months of unanswered e-mails, ignored voice mails, and rescheduled dates, they finally gave you the meeting. Your PowerPoint was something a marketing professional would have been proud of. Your facts were solid. The data you collected spoke to every need the company had. You were textbook with your WIIFM (What's In It For Me?). Your close…mic drop. The room goes silent as your underwhelmed audience says, "Thanks for coming. We'll be in touch." Right there, you felt it.

Maybe it was that girl/boy back in your school days that you had hopes of making your boo. Never mind the fact that you knew you weren't the finest thing walking the hallways or on campus. You finally got the nerve to put yourself out there. You talked yourself into the insanity of stepping to them and letting them know, "[Gulp] Uh…I like you and was wondering if we can take this to the next level." They smiled, and for a nanosecond, for some deranged reason, you think, *This is it! I'm about to win!* A look of puppy-dog awe covers their face as they touch you on the shoulder and say, "I'm sorry, but I don't like you like that. We should probably just be friends." Right there, you felt it.

There's one more person this book is for. The individual that talks themselves out of the game before it even begins. To quote the great Pai Mei, "No wonder you can't do it. You acquiesce to defeat before you even begin." You'd be surprised the life lessons you learn from a watching a Quentin Tarantino joint. Back to my point. When you do this, you give your competition a free pass because you've already assumed you'd get an *L*. Right there, you felt it.

What is that feeling? The obvious answer is rejection. On the contrary, rejection is not a feeling; it's an event. Rejection can be the *source* of several feelings. The feeling of being:

- Inadequate,
- Unappreciated,
- Less than,
- Devalued,
- Insecure,
- Expendable,
- Inferior.

If any of these scenarios resonated with you or if you have your own unique situation that elicited a similar feeling, I got you covered. You're the reason I wrote this book. You and I have something in common. We're "underdogs" in some fashion. I put that in quotes because it's actually a perception. We see ourselves as underdogs, and so we act according to those thoughts, forcing our audience to treat us like an underdog. Conversely, we have an inner burning to show the world that we belong on the big stage. We're not looking for a handout. We don't mind working for what we want. We rarely, however, have the inside track. We've seen others who were/are less deserving occupy a position of prestige with little regard for the honor of being there, and we scream out in agony, "WHY. NOT. ME?" Like I said, I got you covered. This book is for the person that has wondered why someone else was chosen and they weren't. This is me leveling the playing field.

Now on the flip side, if you've gotten this far in reading this yet you find that you can't relate, that's perfectly all right. Again, I appreciate you picking up the book and putting forth this much effort. I mean that sincerely. However, I would ask that you consider this thought: even luxury vehicles need an oil change on a regular basis. I hear you though—"My car runs on battery." Oh yeah? Tell me what happens if you don't keep your battery charged. I'll wait. That's right.

It will die. There's something in here for you too. Imagine super-charging your academic pedigree. The landscape is getting more and more competitive. If you haven't already, you'll soon find that you, too, need something other than those three letters following your name or the panache of a respected institution of higher learning. I'm all for academics, and I appreciate the technical savvy that's gained from a college education. The problem is that some people think academia is all that's needed. GPA alone isn't enough to get you across every finish line, homie. That's real talk. But who am I to make such a claim? After all, I'm a college dropout. Consider TalentSmart, the world's #1 leader in emotional intelligence and the research they've conducted. They concluded, "When emotional intelligence first appeared to the masses in 1995, it served as the missing link in a peculiar finding: people with average IQs outperform those with the highest IQs 70 percent of the time." Yep, it's like that, fam. I know no one else will tell you that your game can use an upgrade. They don't want to hurt your feelings. Truth is, they're telling someone else about your blind spots; they just don't have the nerve to tell you! Not to worry. I'm that person that will let you know you have a booger in your nose. Yeah, it's gross to point out, and it makes for an uncomfortable exchange. My thinking is *Shame on all the other people that saw it and let you walk around looking nasty.* A gross exaggeration, both literally and figuratively, but that's my coaching style. I'm that person to point out what others won't. I care enough that you're not hindered by a miniscule blemish in your game that will ultimately keep you on the bench. In the long run, the ugly truth is better than a beautiful lie.

Let's be honest, none of that matters if the time you invest in reading this book provides no ROI (return on investment)—sorry, that's my financial professional side wanting a little bit of shine. You need to know, and you're well within your rights to know what you're going to get out of committing to these pages. If I were you, I'd want to know too. Plain and simple: you're going to walk away with a competitive advantage you can use in school, in the corporate environment, in your own business, and in your personal life. What does that look like? One thing I'm not talking about is changing who you are at the core. You are who you are and that's a wrap! What *Corporate Swagger* will do for you is create multiple facets of your personality that you can leverage in any given space to compete on a stage where you need to stand out among your peers. Imagine having the confidence of a high-caliber athlete. Visualize yourself with the power to move an audience like a Grammy-award-winning performer. Envision a fearless version of yourself that embraces the challenges that others scurry away from. Picture yourself impervious to the pain of rejection because you now have a defense mechanism that when employed, sustains your dignity rather than depletes it. "Laying it on kind of thick, Rod." I hear you. I'm living proof that what you're about to learn works…if you work it. At some point in time, many of us have danced with the inferiority complex. The impostor syndrome is almost as rampant as the common cold. Everyone's confidence gets shaken. Personally, I still hate rejection, and I'm not alone. I interviewed several others that can attest to the same thing. You'll have an opportunity, just as I have, to glean from their wisdom and apply some of their best practices.

My commitment to you is the same as I give to any audience I'm privileged to address. I promise that your time spent with me on this journey will provide you with tools you can use immediately. Everything I share with you will come from one of my three pillars of thought: experience, wisdom, or fact. I use these pillars for one reason—they can't be disputed. Pillar number one is *experience*. I lived it. I either learned a lesson from doing it wrong or achieved a level of success from doing it right. Either way, it happened to me, and there's no argument that can discredit it. I'll share these experiences with you and the lesson learned from each one.

Pillar number two is *wisdom*. I gathered valuable insight from someone with more credibility or success than me either directly or indirectly. There's an imitator in all of us. It started early in our childhood. We see, we do. There are several people I admire so much that I imitate some part of their game and make it my own. I'll introduce you to some of them in this book. They will share, firsthand, some of their wisdom that you'll be able to add to your repertoire. It worked for them. It worked for me. It will work for you as well.

Pillar number three is *fact*. Look, two plus two is four even in a foreign country. Some things aren't so cerebral that they need to be deeply pondered before being accepted as truth. Wear a wrinkled shirt to work enough times, and people will think you're lazy. Get the reputation of being chronically late, and you'll be labeled unreliable. Those are just facts! In this section I bring in either research that amplifies the subject, statistics that back up the claim, or common-sense principles that prove the point. As in the other pillars, the facts can't be disputed.

Now that the formalities are out of the way, let's get it! You see, every game has players, an objective, and rules. The players and objective are usually very clear. It's the explanation and understanding of the rules that are often vague. Your desired outcome depends heavily on the full disclosure of these rules, your level of understanding, and the degree to which you bend these rules in your favor. Consider this your tool to do just that. With this you'll be equipped to manipulate the parameters of a once-unfair game. These pages have yet to be included in any college textbook. You haven't attended this lecture class. This is the competitive advantage that makes the average worker professionally attractive. This is why others were chosen and you weren't. This guide has been well guarded until now. Some call it the "X" factor. Other refer to it as having "it." I like to refer to it as *Corporate Swagger: The Secrets to Winning the Corporate Game*. Lace 'em up. It's game time.

CHAPTER 1

. . . .

You vs. You

"Don't let fear stop you from doing the thing you love."

—Buster Moon,
the koala from the movie *Sing*

Think back to when you were a child. Recall that toy, the new shoes, or the dollhouse you had your heart set on. It may have been something so big and outrageous that you never shared your desire with anyone—it was a *secret petition.* It was so big that you knew if you let the cat out of the bag, you'd risk getting laughed at or rejected. That potential ridicule didn't stop it from consuming your thoughts to the extent that you imagined how to get it, what you would do once you got it, and how you'd tell the tale to those who asked. Then one day out of the blue, that kid from down the street gets the same toy you wanted. Your classmate comes to school in the kicks you imagined wearing. Your cousin invites you over to play with the dollhouse you fantasized about. Now you're older and you find yourself reliving this nightmare. Only now, like some kind of menacing virus, it's oozed its way into your professional life. It's time-out for sitting idly by while others gallivant across the finish line with arms raised in victory while you sit there agonizing over another failed attempt. But as the saying goes, "Don't hate the player. Hate the game." I won't insist that I know exactly how they came out on top. I can guarantee you this though: at the very least, they put themselves in position by winning the first battle of Corporate Swagger—the battle of the mind.

I referenced it earlier, but there's a line in the movie *Kill Bill: Vol. 2* that illustrates this perfectly. If you haven't seen the movie, allow me to explain. If you have, just go with me here. Uma Thurman's character, Beatrix Kiddo, is being groomed to be an assassin. She has decent fighting skills, but she needs an upgrade for the kind of work she's about to be assigned. Bill, her handler (played by David Carradine), drops her off to be trained by a Shaolin monk and kung fu master by the name of Pai Mei. He's that cat everyone needs on their squad…just in case it goes down and you need someone who's nice with them hands or, in his case, hands and feet. During her training with Pai Mei, he instructs her to punch through this wooden wall about five inches thick while only having her fist three inches away from it. She can't wind up with her torso and throw her entire body weight into the punch as you would normally do. She can't bend her elbow back behind her as you would in a typical punching motion. She's restricted to a three-inch window of space between her and the wall. From that distance, she had to create enough force to put her fist through the wood as if it were a piece of paper. The point in this exercise is found in the question she's asked by the Shaolin monk, "What if your enemy is three inches in front of you? What do you do then?" After assessing the degree of difficulty, she shrinks into a yielding mind-set. She follows that up with a pitiful excuse for why she couldn't do it. Then Pai Mei delivers a line that most of us have heard some version of ourselves. With a ferocity fueled with disgust for such a weak submission, he says, "No wonder you can't do it. You acquiesce to defeat before you even begin."

How many times do we count ourselves out before we even start? Walter D. Wintle put it beautifully in his poem, "The Man Who Thinks He Can": "If you think you're beaten, you are. If you think you'll lose, you've lost." I'm not dropping fresh philosophy here—I was a music major. Philosophy wasn't my thing, but the question is worth pondering. Why do we allow ourselves to fall victim to this mental bully? I submit to you that it's because we erroneously identify the opponent as the wall in front of us. The true advisory isn't the wall. Scientifically, it's the neurons that are transmitting signals in that 40/60 combination of gray-and-white matter that make up your brain. In laymen's terms, the true advisory is your thoughts. In the hood you'd be told to "Get-cha mind right!"

If you can't win this battle, then all you've done is make a much-appreciated donation to the Rodney S. Jones Fund. That's my way of saying this purchase was futile, this book won't help you, and you've wasted your time. As much as I'd like to say otherwise, unless you can punch through this wall, eventually you'll curl up in a ball and give in to defeat before you even try. Failure here makes all remaining lessons ineffective, and this will be just another book you've read and got nothing from. These pages can and will only provide so much help. Ultimately, you must decide that you are going to win this epic battle of you vs. you.

EXPERIENCE

Ask me what I wanted to be when I grew up and without hesitation, I would have told you, "I want to be in the NBA." No surprise there. Many kids grow up with aspirations of playing professional sports. As I moved through middle school and then high school, that dream began to get more and more faint. I turned out to be a choir boy (and damned proud of it!) and not a varsity athlete. I tried out for the middle-school team and was able to make the seventh-grade B-team. I tried out later for high-school varsity but only got as far as the tenth-grade B-team. I took one more shot at the varsity team, but I guess I didn't have enough of what the coach was looking for. None of that had any impact on my affinity for the game. Despite not making it to the pinnacle of organized scholastic sports, I still loved playing and would do so any time I had the chance. I never turned down an opportunity to hoop. When time permitted, there was no place I'd rather be than on a random court around town getting in a pickup game with friends or complete strangers. When I got to college, the pickup games had a little more at stake—ego and reputation. In my mind I couldn't afford to give anyone reason to believe my game was whack. I didn't need the additional ridicule and validation from anyone else that I wasn't good enough to play. Nevertheless, the fantasy of being in the NBA eventually dissipated. Who was I kidding? The natural first step before going pro is to be on a college team. The closest I got to playing college ball was playing on the same gym floor with guys that eventually did go pro.

As it would turn out, the opportunity presented itself. Written in the campus newspaper were the words "Open Tryout." The head coach of the Longhorn basketball team decided to open things up and give anyone on campus who thought they could play a shot at being on the team. Didn't matter if you played high school ball. Didn't matter if you played pickup ball. If you thought you had game, the door was open to prove it. This was it! My redemption song was playing, and this choir boy was ready to sing. At least that's how it goes in fairytale land. No sooner than I read those two words did I tell myself there was no way I would get picked. Like I had suddenly gained enough skills to go from the tenth-grade B-team to making a Division I college basketball team—yeah right! Not a chance. Every time I think about it, I get mad at myself. All I had to do was show up. Show 'em how wet the jumper can be. Let 'em see the defense I could play. It wasn't "lockdown" defense but it was "Don't get embarrassed out here" defense. Not your boy though. I lost the battle.

One Saturday afternoon months after the open tryouts, I was watching a Longhorn basketball game and I saw him. I saw this guy we all used to play pickup ball with on campus. I watched him leave the bench and check into the game. He was on TV! He was playing for the Horns! He had tried out and made the team! He saw the same ad in the newspaper that I did. This was the same dude I used to play ball with at the REC. As a matter of fact, we had played ball together a couple weeks ago. From what I had witnessed up close, his jumper wasn't wet, handle wasn't tight, and he was not a lockdown defender. How in the crap had he made the team? This guy was someone that often got picked last. If you know anything about pickup ball, getting picked last is a clear sign that no one wants you on their team. It's the court of public opinion ruling you guilty of having no game. That's the nice way of saying they think you suck. That same court of public opinion would constantly rule that my game was substantially better than his. I never faced the embarrassment of being picked last. Not even close to last. I was the equivalent of a "late first round, early second round" pick. I was always a favorable pick. So how did he make the team? Simple—he won the battle. He didn't let the seed of what others thought of him be planted into his subconscious where it would produce inferior thoughts about himself. He ignored what looked to be obvious. He ignored the comparisons. He ignored the lies. Something in him said, "I don't care who else is trying out. I'm going to go out there and do my best. In the end, I'll be able to hold my head up high and say I tried." He did everything I could have done but didn't do. The result was that I got to watch him for the rest of the year on television. I got to see him around campus in his exclusive team gear. I got to see what life would have possibly looked like had I tried out. No, there's no guarantee I would have made the team. I did guarantee that I *wouldn't* make the team, further solidifying that I'd never play in the NBA. All because I lost the battle before the fight even began. Pai Mei would have been so disappointed in me.

As the famous poet James Todd Smith once wrote, "Don't call it a comeback!" Years later I would have another "you vs. you rematch"; and yes, I was primed for a comeback. This time, I was determined to learn from my mistakes. I was job searching and decided to post for a position that not only required a degree but also a degree in accounting—neither of which I had. Like I said, I was a music major, and due to a familial situation, I decided to forego the rest of my college education to take full legal custody of my two younger sisters. Out of everything in the job description and duties, those were the only two boxes I didn't check. Ironically enough, my thought was *If I can just get an interview, I'll show them I can be just as productive, if not more, than someone who checks* all *the boxes.* Wouldn't you know it? I got the interview! Now the ball was in my court. Do or die. Game time. Put up or shut up. I was given another "open tryout." Fully confident in my strengths yet aware of my shortfall, I knew this position was mine for the taking. Nothing else mattered. My mind was made up. I was walking away with this job. I progressed through the interview process to meet with two levels of management. I'll never forget one of them saying, "You know, you're not qualified on paper, but there's something about you. We're going to hire you." That moment for me was the equivalent of playing in a televised basketball game and hitting the winning jump shot for the championship. That's when I learned how to win the battle. Below is what I did.

Winning the Battle: Step 1—Focus on the Yes

I hear you though. "Yeah, I don't like rejection." Who does? When have you ever heard someone say, "You know what I like? Being told no! When people turn me down, that's the best feeling ever! Give me some more of that!"? We're all sensitive to being rejected. So if everyone would rather avoid rejection, what separates those who show up to the open tryout from those who acquiesce to defeat before they even begin? Those who show up have a super-power. Be excited because you have the same power. This isn't one of those things that is woven into someone's DNA. No, this power can be developed by anyone willing to put forth the effort.

Remember, this is experience talking. I used to fold like a wet piece of paper at any situation that could potentially end up with me being rejected. I still hate rejection to this day! Whereas I used to retreat from those moments, now I charge toward them. What changed? Three simple words became a mainstay in my vernacular. "Why not me?" You've heard people say it. That's just it—they *say* it. So I began asking myself out loud, "Why not me?" Sure, there were answers staring me in the face that pointed to why not. I knew how that story ended, but I wanted different results. I began thinking about the what if. I chose to awaken the daydreamer. My imagination had been in slumber since my childhood days. Back then we had the power to be someone different every day. I recaptured that feeling. It's like the moment when Superman realizes he can fly. The power had been there all along. I just didn't know how to activate it. Don't underestimate the skills you developed in your youth. If it were a job, I'd think about showing up there every day. If it were a goal, I'd spend time imagining hitting it. I'd allow myself to be so captivated by the thoughts that my heartbeat would literally race as if I were living in the moment. I focused on being told yes.

Winning the Battle: Step 2—Redefining Rejection

First, let's look at what rejection does: it leaves you deflated. Rejection is that girl at the party who's dancing by herself. She's having a good time. You make your way next to her, just close enough so that you don't have to scream over the music. You take a sip from that "cup of courage" right before you put yourself out there to ask, "Would you like to dance?" She smiles and says, "No." Rejection is that person that interviews you. You introduce them to your best representative—that version of yourself you send in to make the first impression when you know the regular version of you would jack it up. In the end they smile, shake your hand, and that's it. They go into the witness protection program because you never hear from them again. Ultimately, you're left with that "Call me" feeling like Eddie Murphy in *Boomerang*. Rejection robs you of your dignity. It invokes a feeling of not being good enough. Rejection grabs the megaphone and blares to the deepest recesses of your ear canal, " You're. Not. Worthy!" When it happens, you walk away with a little less of yourself than when you showed up. So what are your options? You can live your life avoiding rejection, or you can find a way to deal with it.

What does it mean to redefine rejection? It means exactly that. Change what rejection means to you. It's like the word *bad* meaning something good. The word *phat* (spelled with a *p*) not meaning *overweight*. You can choose to make the word mean whatever you want it to mean. Believe that new meaning then act accordingly. I've redefined rejection this way: They didn't reject me; I've simply eliminated an option. Here's the logic behind the new definition. In most (if not all) opportunities out there, you're only looking for the best *one*. Amid all the possibilities lies that *one* perfect scenario—that *one* person, that *one* job, that *one* client. "But, Rodney, I don't want just one. I want all of 'em." If all of 'em were made available to you at one time, you couldn't handle it. Research has been done to prove that even something as small as multitasking will eventually result in inefficiency and error. You can build up to handling multiple opportunities later; right now you just need the *one*.

Remember, every flood starts with a single raindrop. Before there was an avalanche, there was a solitary snowflake. Your job is to quickly identify the pesky inhibitors that will subsequently chart a clear path to your yes. Yes, it's contrary to all things common sense, but relying on the norm has kept you at bay. By using the process of elimination, you eventually get to your destination—the yes. When you change how you define rejection, hearing no becomes a good thing. It means that's one less thing impeding your progress, putting you well on your way to getting the answer you want. If that's the case, you should want to be told no early and often so you can get your yes sooner rather than later. In doing this you'll also realize is that you're in control of this little experiment. It's as if you're the one making the final decision. Since you're in control, getting rejected doesn't hurt as much. You get to retain a lot more of your dignity than if you put yourself at the mercy of someone else making the decision. Eliminate that feeling and there you have it. You've given new meaning to rejection.

Imagine a forty-story office building with an office on each floor. Each office has a gatekeeper. Only one of these gatekeepers has a golden ticket. You're tasked with asking each gatekeeper if they have the golden ticket until you find the one that does. At first glance this seems like a daunting task—trivial even. You think to yourself, *That's a lot of offices. It will take me forever to go ask every gatekeeper if they have the golden ticket.* Then you sink deeper into that defeated mentality when your analytical tendencies kick in: 40 - 1 = 39. Forty offices minus one ticket equals thirty-nine times you can get rejected. This math doesn't lie. It forces you to start justifying why you shouldn't even give it a shot. *Who needs a golden ticket anyway? I'm good with the tattered-up ticket I already have. I don't want to be told no that many times.*

Then you remember to redefine rejection. Your thinking changes. Your analytical tendencies create a different equation. Instead you compute that 40 - 39 = 1. Your thoughts tell you, *There are forty offices, and I get to eliminate thirty-nine of them. When I do that, I'm guaranteed to walk away with one golden ticket.* New motivation creates an excitement. This newfound enthusiasm causes you to get this mischievous "Grinch stole Christmas" smile on your face because you realize you have a competitive advantage. In the end, you're going to win. You're walking away from this search victorious. The only thing left is to begin the process of elimination. You ask the first gatekeeper, "Do you have the golden ticket?" Imagine the poise when you ask. Borderline smug if you will. The first gatekeeper says no. Rejection stares you in the face once again, but something is different this time. Despite being told no, you're off to the next office with your dignity intact. Your head is held high. Your posture strangely resembles that of someone that was given good news. Why? Because you've redefined rejection. Your thinking has changed. On your way to the next office, you whisper to yourself, "They didn't reject me. I eliminated an option."

WISDOM

Every battle starts in the mind. When it comes to being successful, what are some of your strategies to stay mentally tough?

I chose to seek the wisdom of people who have proven to be victorious when it comes to this battle. You'll be interested to know that I found three prevailing themes in response to this question. None of what they shared with me was rocket science, but all of it worked for them and it was easily executed. It comes down to anchoring yourself in your core values, the software you're running, and having mental bandwidth.

I have this saying, "If two people say your breath stink and they've never spoken to each other, you might want to grab a mint." When reviewing my notes from the interviews I conducted, it was an overwhelming conclusion that having a strong mental game started with having clearly defined core values. This notion first came about when I when I talked to Tyra Metoyer. I was in my office during a lunch break when we linked up for this conversation. The sixty minutes I spent on the phone with her gave me a fresh perspective on my own professional track. Tyra is the senior director for community engagement and corporate responsibility for a consumer electronics company. Tyra's schooling includes an undergraduate degree from The University of Texas where she studied journalism, public relations, advertising, and applied communication; a master's degree in community development from Prairie View A&M University; and a PhD in higher education from Texas A&M University. Tyra is a natural problem solver. She's gifted in that area and flexes that muscle daily. To be proficient at solving problems, her mental game must stay on point. Her answer is to understand who you are and what's important to you. That's found in your core values. Not the answer I was expecting, but then I talked to one of my fraternity brothers, Joseph Norman.

Joe had just taken an assignment in Canada weeks before we got together, so we decided to make good use of technology and make ours a video call. Joe and I went to different colleges but in the same city. He attended Huston-Tillotson University, an HBCU, at the same time I was at UT. He graduated with a BS in computer science and mathematics. His seventeen-year stint with IBM had that " 🎵 started from the bottom now we here" theme music playing the background. He started as a staff software engineer / team lead and worked his way up to program director, global escalations and SWAT engineering. Yeah, I didn't know what that meant either until he broke it down to me. He said, "I spent the past ten years working in a high-stressed environment because I deal with pissed-off people on a daily basis." You would think the way he stayed mentally tough would be something similar to the mediation method of a Monk, but no. Just the same as Tyra, Joe told me the key is having a core sense of who you are and knowing what's important to you. That's just two people. Then it happened again.

Sarah Bolka, a former Marine Corps officer, fellow board member for Big Brothers Big Sisters of America (Houston region) and nine-year commercial professional for ExxonMobil said the same thing. Usually, we attribute Marine wisdom to the battlefield. Sarah's answer was an echo of what I had previously heard, "Trust yourself. Trust your preparation. And know your core values." She went on to explain that when she can anchor herself on unshakable core values, it gives her the freedom to go after something unapologetically. They're all right. When you have a clearly defined line of values, it's like setting a thermostat. You don't have to worry as much about the environment you're in or the situation you're going to face because eventually it will all give way to temperature you've set. That temperature is your core values.

Next let's tackle this concept of the software you're running. I'm not talking about your cell phone or your desktop/laptop. There's a hard drive that houses much more sensitive data than either of those. I'm referring to your HOS (Human Operating System). It's imperative to make sure your software is not only up to date but also protected from malware. What do I mean? Your mind is the hard drive. The things we take in verbally, visually, and audibly are the software. Malware is any outside information that can corrupt your thinking. Our output, or how we respond to any given situation, depends entirely on the data stored in our minds. We have to recall from somewhere. That recall is determined by the things we say, hear, and see.

Steven and Finesia Coleman are a married couple with a robust business in the financial industry. Steven's degree in criminal justice from Texas A&M Commerce somehow led to nearly two decades of entrepreneurial experience in a competitive sector. Their day-to-day success hinges on winning this battle. Together they've created a legacy for their family and have helped to impact the lives of countless others. I met Steven at one of his Houston locations. There in his office we talked, and he shared with me that you have to be able to trick your mind into believing the things conducive to being successful. Sounds about right for a former collegiate track athlete. He went on to explain that controlling your thoughts, environment, and experiences is the way to do that. Sounds like a software update to me. It's recognizing when the data you have available to recall is not yielding the desired results and making the necessary adjustments. Sounds like that Beyoncé joint, "Let-me-let-me upgrade ya!" He went on to say that the other end of this scenario rings true as well. If you grow up your whole life in negative situations, you'll have to snuff out all the bad thinking to even see yourself as successful. That's what I call a data wipe.

Based on my "stinky breath" theory, we need someone else to express the same thing for it to be true, right? That brings me to my conversation with Veronica Brooks, a former colleague of mine in New York. She's more than qualified to speak on this topic considering her path to success started in Watts, Los Angeles—yeah, that Watts. No doubt that her mind-set had to be in the right place to go from there to Barnard College where she got her degree in economics to getting her MBA in finance, leadership, and marketing from Columbia Business School to becoming a successful marketing communication professional within financial services. And to top it all off, she's an emerging author. She shared with me that her best practice is (1) envisioning what she wants her day to look like based on what she wants to achieve. Google "visualization for athletes," and you'll see that this practice is highly touted to improve sports performance. Spoiler alert: you don't have to be a professional athlete to use it. Second, Veronica makes it a habit to speak positive words of affirmation over herself. She told me she has a list of adjectives at her desk that she can quickly reference to make sure she's in the right frame of mind.

Let's say the visualization thing is too progressive for you. Really doesn't matter because there are different names for the same principle. I figured that out after talking with Anthony Rosette. I've had the privilege of gleaning from this man since my college days and well into my professional years. Anthony is another University of Texas graduate with a bachelor of science in mechanical engineering. He's a PMI-certified project management professional with more than fifteen years of experience driving globally distributed development projects in natural gas trading, upstream oil production, energy services, financial trading and high tech. That alone is enough to convince me that he's doing things that require a near-flawless mental game. During our phone conversation, I asked him the same question, and he didn't hesitate to tell me he's always functioned with the mind-set of beginning with the end in mind. In his line of work, he depends on something he calls exit criteria. It's derived from another phrase in his industry called acceptance criteria. Acceptance criteria are the conditions that need to be met on your way to completing a project. When all the boxes have been checked, the other party will accept what you've delivered. This process of checks and balances allows you to move from one phase to another. What Anthony does at the beginning of each day is set an exit criteria for himself. It's his way of defining the things that need to be done in order produce an expected deliverable. Sound familiar? Call it what you want—visualization, beginning with the end in mind, exit criteria, doing the hokeypokey, whatever. The principle is the same: manage the software of your human operating system.

The other theme that kept coming up in responses to this question had to do with increasing your bandwidth. Simply put, you have to always work to increase your knowledge base. On a sunny Houston day outside of a Barnes & Noble, dripped in Pittsburgh Steelers gear, sipping on a strawberry acai lemonade, my sister-in-law began to spit the actual factual on her approach to mind-set. "You have to create yourself a 'superpower,' which means knowing more than everyone else," she said. Byrena Washington used this "superpower" to help her go from line cook to culinary partner to her current role of assistant operating partner at P. F. Chang's China Bistro. From the beginning of her career, she made it a point to take the initiative to learn what others wouldn't teach her. It was that kind of initiative that earned her the first promotion and the same initiative that prompted her to return to school to get her MBA from American Intercontinental University. It was funny to hear that colleagues call her the P. F. Chang's dictionary. That kind of reputation speaks to the depth of her knowledge and applauds the effort she took to gain it.

That takes me to my conversation with Thoma Brewer, another UT alum. Thoma earned a BA in ethnic studies and business foundations. For the past four years, he's served as the director of corporate training and people resources at the College of Health Care Professions. His role spans the breadth from culture management to employee relations to budget management to training and development—all of which demand him to stay at the top of his mental game. Yet he echoes the same thing. Thoma told me he evaluates what he knows and doesn't know and acknowledges it pretty quickly. To account for his blind spots, he has a myriad of tactics. The dusky lounge in a quaint part of town made for the perfect setting for the story he told me. Watching him take debonair sips of Crown and Coke had me feeling like I was sitting at the feet of the Godfather or something. He began to tell me how he was in a meeting with some of the company's top brass. Some of them included financial professionals who were throwing around a bunch of shop talk and jargon that he wasn't familiar with. Staying true to his process, he cleverly took out his phone and googled the terminology they were using to get a better understanding. Once his "download" was complete, he interjected his $0.02, and no one was the wiser that he had just upgraded his software right in front of them.

In addition to on-the-spot updates to his HOS, he also maximizes his connections. Thoma takes advantage of every opportunity to learn from others, whether he knows them or not. He explained that he takes the time to ask colleagues about their role and how it impacts the business. Thoma even leverages outside relationships—those beyond the four walls of work—to gain mental advantages. He'll take an experience that he learns about in his social circle and use that intel to navigate workplace situations. One thing he mentioned that sounds repetitive but rings true is that he reads a lot of business journals. I once heard that if you want to hide something from a black person, put it in a book. These days, that statement no longer has a racial bias. More and more people are ignoring the wealth of information available at their fingertips. Thoma makes sure to get information in every possible way to ensure that when the moment comes, he's ready.

The most interesting response to the same question came during my conversation with Darryl Blackburn. I first met Darryl at a board of directors meeting for the Houston region of Big Brothers Big Sisters of America. Even though we sit on the same side of philanthropy and community service, we went to college on opposing sides of the Red River—he's a Sooner, I'm a Longhorn. That withstanding, it didn't take long for me to see that he's a prized fighter in the "you vs. you" battle. For that reason, I had to sit down with him to see how he did it. He graduated with his bachelor of science in petroleum engineering and flexes that muscle at a prestigious oil-and-gas company in Houston, Texas, where he serves as a petroleum engineer. We met up after work hours at a spot tucked away in the Houston Heights. I asked him the same question. His answer closely resembled what I had been hearing, but he delivered it differently. He said, "Put in the time to learn the minutia. Really successful people descend into the particulars." He explained that when you know about the smallest details, then by nature, you'll be mentally tougher than other people in that space. To do this, Darryl believes in turning his car into his classroom. During his commute into the office, he's not listening to music or sports radio. Instead, he's soaking up information that keeps him mentally sharp. Don't get me wrong. He enjoys his sports. As an Oklahoma alum and native Houstonian, he gets it in. But for the most part, he's constantly in student mode. His reason is clear. In his words, "The more information you surround yourself with, the fewer conversations you'll find yourself to be unqualified for."

I'll put a bow on it with an additional piece of wisdom Veronica shared with me: Knowledge builds wisdom. Wisdom builds confidence. Confidence helps you to handle a full spectrum of different situations. Constant exposure to those multiple spectrums builds growth (because you step out in courage). Growth builds mental toughness. Like I said, "Better get-cha mind right!"

FACT

The late executive director of the United Negro College Fund, Arthur Fletcher, was credited with coining the phrase "A mind is a terrible thing to waste." How do we waste our mind's potential? When we fail to tap into its awesome power. We have tangible proof of the wondrous power of the mind when we allow it to imagine possibilities that push the boundaries of what seems improbable. In fact, we call a few of them Wonders of the World. The mind created the Taj Mahal with its stunning beauty that attracts millions of visitors each year. The mind created the largest amphitheater in the world, more commonly known as The Colosseum. Its magnificence is validated by the fact that of all the buildings that don the name *colosseum*, this one is known as *the* Colosseum. Before it sat on top of the Corcovado Mountain, Christ the Redeemer in Brazil was in someone's mind. The mind created the Great Wall of China and the Pyramid of Giza. Might I remind you that each of these Wonders of the World was created in a time before the technology and machinery we have today. That means it was done with limited resources. One resource stands the test of time: the power to imagine a thing into existence.

Fact: we can choose to either employ the power of our mind or be employed by that same power. Consider two people that grew up under the same negative circumstances: abuse, drugs, alcohol, poverty. One person has constant thoughts of escaping this way of living and never returning. Day in and day out this person thinks about the possibilities of living a better life. There's no way to deny their current situation, but they refuse to let it become a permanent occupant of space in their mind. This person's battle cry is "When I get out of here…" Not for one minute do they think about the *if*. For them, it's all about the *when*. They focus on the yes.

Contrast that with the other person in the same situation. They've chosen to be employed by the power of their mind. Like a boat with a hole, they take it all in with the looming expectation of sinking. They allow circumstances to guide their thoughts. In a sense, they focus on the no. Consequently, their thoughts produce negative words that give birth to self-defeating actions. Unlike their counterpart, *when* is never an option. Mustering up enough hope to even think about the *if* is too much to consider. It's no surprise why one of them makes it to their version of paradise and the other remains captive to the environment saturated with negativity. The difference is clear. One chose to employ and the other chose to be employed.

The power of the mind is evident when we look at the placebo effect. Question: how is it that a person can undergo surgery with no anesthesia and exhibit very little sign of pain? Answer: when the patient (unbeknownst to him) is injected with saltwater instead of morphine and they were tricked into believing they were given a painkiller. Without knowing any better, they chose to believe the substance flowing through their veins would numb the pain. The belief produced a result of minimal discomfort on the part of the patient. Imagine wielding the kind of power that allows you to say, "Just give me a cup of water, Doc, and I'll be good to go. Once this H_2O kicks in, you can go ahead with the surgery." Fact: We get to choose what we believe. The results stem from actions that are rooted in thoughts. Don't like the results you're getting? Check your thought patterns. It's simple, like 2 + 2 = 4; thoughts + actions = results. Increase the first variable, and the result has to follow suit. Better thoughts make for better results.

The biggest battle you will ever fight is with yourself. Joyce Meyer calls it the battlefield of the mind. This is where the fight begins. This is where you either claim your victory or submit to defeat. We've proven how powerful the mind is when employed to work for you. We've also shown how equally powerful it is when it's allowed to call the shots. This lesson is the bedrock for everything else you will read here. It's so important that I've given you a few exercises to get you ready for what you're about to learn. It's paramount that you understand the gravity of this concept. I implore you. Do not proceed to any of the other chapters until you can honestly win the battle of you vs. you.

CALL TO ACTION

Here's an exercise for you. This is something I've prescribed to all my coaching clients who suffer at the hands of a defeated mind-set. The purpose of this activity is to get you to think differently about who you are. You need to understand that you belong. This is the core reason why most people lose the battle—they don't believe they belong. I've done this myself, and it worked. It will work for you too. There are three options.

Option 1: The Test Drive

Go test-drive a car that's outside of your budget. Hold on before you go out there and get your face cracked. I need you to do some work first. You need to do some extensive research. I need you to know just as much about this automobile as the person selling it. Understand all the minute details, know about the different options, even study the maker. Once you've done your homework, then it's time to prepare for the conversation. There's one question that can throw a monkey wrench in the whole program: "So what do you do for a living?" Understand the question behind the question. What they really want to know is, Will you be able to handle the financial responsibility? If that's the case, you don't necessarily have to answer the surface question. Answer the underlying question. There are several ways people come into money: investing, saving, inheritance, owning a business. Find a safe answer that works best for you and one that won't put you in a compromising position. Don't lie because they'll smell that from a mile away.

I test-drove a $98K Range Rover when my account was in the negative. When the sales rep asked me the same question, my response was "I'm in the financial industry." Never mind the fact that I was hemorrhaging for sales and I had no money in my account. When you've done your homework and you're prepared to answer any personal questions, the last piece to this puzzle is looking the part. I need you to understand your audience. We'll dig deeper into this later. You may need to put on your Sunday best. Whatever it takes. When in Rome, do as Romans do. Now it's time to make the visit. You won't have to work hard to get someone to talk to you because as soon as you step on to the lot, they can smell you. Pace yourself. Don't get too excited. You'll need to converse with the salesperson for a minute to prove you know something about the car/maker before exposing your true intentions. When the time is right and the conversation has brought you to the right moment, that's when you say, "Yeah, I think I'd like to take it out for a spin. I'd like to get a feel for it myself to see if it's really like what I've heard." The goal is to have an experience that you think is reserved for a select few. Once you're test-driving this automobile that's out of your current budget, you'll realize that if you think you belong, you'll have corresponding actions that will produce results beyond your expectations. When you think you belong, others will treat you as if you *do* belong.

Option 2: Dress Rehearsal Shopping

If the first option is too much for you right now, no problem. Here's a version that provides the same experience but on a smaller stage. There's window-shopping, then there's actual shopping. This is what happens in between. Make a trip to an upscale shopping mall or boutique. You're looking for an apparel store—any item of clothing will work: shoes, clothes, accessories (ties, purses, etc.). Not as much research is required for this option, but it wouldn't hurt to know a little something about the background of the maker and brand behind the product. Proving to be knowledgeable never hurts. Same as before, you'll need to look the part. For this activity to flow smoothly, you'll need to adopt this phrase: "That's not bad." You'll have to force yourself to use this phrase anytime you feel the urge to cringe at a price outside of what you would fathom paying. Your instinct will want to revert to verbiage that proves you don't belong. Verbiage like "😲 Oh! That's expensive!" No, no, no. You can't blow your cover. You have to talk like someone who's used to this. A regular patron would not flinch at a $350 necktie or a $700 wallet, so neither should you. With the utmost finesse, they'd nod their head in agreement and say, "That's not bad." That's if they said anything at all. Remember, you must respond with this phrase instinctually. Once you're ready, choose the store and pick an item of clothing to try on. Look at yourself in the mirror. Enjoy the moment.

If you're looking the part, the salesperson should ask you some sort of closing question like "Would you like me to bag that up for you?"

To which, you'll respond (unless you want to buy it), "No thanks. It didn't fit like I thought it would." If it's an accessory, "No thanks. I'm not sure it will go with the outfit I'm looking to wear with it." Return the items to the salesperson and exit stage left. What have you done? You've proven that you belong. You've infiltrated the secret club. You know the password and now you're in. All you've really done is changed your thinking, taken corresponding actions, and gotten different results.

Option 3: This Is My House

This one is simple. It's like the previous exercises but requires no research and no phrases to remember. Simply find an affluent part of town where there are homes for sale. The more expensive, the better. I suggest something above the $500K mark. When I first did this, it was with a $1MM home. Many places will have a realtor offering tours of the property—an open house. This exercise is all about imagination. I don't want you to just walk through the home. That won't accomplish the objective. I need you to act as if this home was yours—with a level of decorum, of course. After all, this isn't your home, so don't do anything too far-fetched. If the first thing you do when you get (to your actual) home is open the refrigerator, then walk into this home and make a beeline to the kitchen and open the refrigerator. Walk into the master bedroom and plop down on the bed. Go into the closet and imagine your clothes hanging there. Where would you put your shoes? Motion as if you were taking a pair down. Where would you sit to put them on? Sit in that spot. Literally go through the motions. This is all about taking your mind to a place enough times that it becomes familiar. When the thought is a familiar thought, the actions will be second nature and the results will be to your liking. This is how you win the battle of you vs. you.

CHAPTER 2

. . . .

Friend or Foe

"Ain't nobody dope as me / I'm dressed so fresh so clean."

—Outkast

#TBT: Go back to your middle school or high school days. Remember the night before the first day of school? For most people, this was the most important day of the year. It had nothing to do with the school supplies, classes, or the teachers. It had everything to do with what you were going to wear. The gravity of this decision had stock market-like ramifications on your social currency for the remainder of the school year. Come correct, and you were guaranteed access into the "A-crowd." Mess this up, and you became the punch line of every joke for the rest of the school year. It was critical that you have the right shoes and the perfect shirt—and don't even get me started on the hair. It had to be flawless—I'm talking Mortal Kombat. Some of us even went through the process of laying everything out on the bed the night before. We'd step back, give the one-dimensional ensemble a once over, and say, "I'm go'n kill 'em tomorrow! They ain't ready!"

Why did we put so much equity into that moment? Even at an early age, without attending a professional development training course, instinctively, we understood the importance of appearance. Albeit for superficial reasons, the principle is the same now: how we look matters. It speaks before we have a chance to utter a word. It communicates without our full participation. It's the perpetual billboard on the highway of our lives. Most importantly, our appearance gives others a filter to see us through. This goes for emerging professionals, entrepreneurs, and seasoned veterans alike. Now that you've graduated, the setting may have changed, but the game hasn't. The school has evolved into an office building. Jeans and sneakers have switched to tailored suits and dress shoes. Backpacks are now briefcases. Classrooms have transformed into plush conference rooms. Overwhelmingly, you no longer want the attention of the cute boy/girl that sat next to you. Your aim is to get the attention of senior management. Same game. The stakes just got higher.

EXPERIENCE

Gambling is not my forte. I know this because I almost lost everything when I bet on academia's definition of proper work attire. No textbook, no lecture class, not even the career services center at the flagship university I attended prepared me for what I'm about to share with you. I had no idea there was an underlying meaning to this cliché we've all accepted as the golden rule for professional attire. You know it. C'mon, say it with me. "Dress…to…impress." My understanding of dressing professional for work meant "wear a suit and you'll be respected." It was the minimum standard. There was no other option. You may have had a different experience, but mine was such that I left college believing there was no other way to dress for work. The role was irrelevant. What mattered was showing up in a suit. Even if it was a ~~Broke~~ Brooks Brothers suit—you'll get that later.

So there I was fresh off the Forty Acres. I landed what I would call my first grown-up job. I acquired it through what was considered typical channels. I posted my résumé on a reputable career site, received interest from the employer, had a phone screen followed by a round of interviews. After a waiting period, I received a phone call from an office representative letting me know I had the job. Somewhere in the conversation I know they mentioned the pay, but all I heard was $30,000/year. I'm sure this person gave me some additional information about that number, but I tuned out soon after I heard it. I was instant rich! My limited thinking would have never fathomed I'd earn that much money in a year. In my mind, this had to be the biggest heist ever pulled off by a college dropout. This was it! I finally made it into the professional ranks. The office representative continued with details surrounding my attendance for the ensuing training class. Then she did the unthinkable. She messed around and told me that a flight and hotel would be reserved for me. 😲 WHAT! I was stompin' with the BIG DOGS!

My first day of training was when I realized what I didn't pay attention to during that initial phone conversation. The salary they mentioned was something called first-year earning potential. Yeah, I had agreed to a 100 percent commission-based role straight out of school. Did I mention I had two other mouths to feed? The whole reason for this job search was because I had just taken full legal custody of my two younger sisters. Here I was in a new city, new apartment, with two dependents and working in an industry I knew nothing about and getting paid solely based on my performance. So when I said that gambling wasn't my forte because I almost lost it all by betting on academia's version of dressing for success, I meant it. I had no savings, no backup plan, no roommate to hold me down if things got tight…no nothing! So I was pretty much pushing the livelihood of my two sisters in the middle of the table and rolling the dice on what I soon found out was an antiquated meaning of professional attire.

The role was a sales job for an online start-up company. My job was to sell prequalified leads to residential contractors. This is the equivalent to selling ice to an Eskimo—the hardest sale to make. Too late to tuck tail and run. I had two other people depending on me to figure it out. I was given a very simple equation based on this newfound concept of "You eat what you kill." A closed sale meant I was able to get the contractors to sign the agreement. Every time I did that, I would make $200. Based on my expenses, I needed sixteen contractors to sign on that dotted line every month without fail. This would provide me enough to pay bills, keep a roof over our heads, and feed my sisters. Seemed simple enough. However, I knew nothing about the residential contracting industry. The language, the nuances, the mind-set of my audience, how they dressed was all foreign territory to me. All my colleagues had ten to fifteen years of experience in this area, so they were right at home. But hey, I was the cocky college student from UT. What starts here changes the world, right? Wrong. I got my face cracked after every presentation I gave to a potential buyer. I couldn't figure it out. My phone skills were good enough to get them in the door. My presentation was keenly delivered each time—careful to tailor it to the specific needs of the individual. Time after time they would hear me out and leave having passed on my proposal. This went on for a month. Imagine my confusion and desperation.

I had done all the hard work that needed to be done—even more than my coworkers—but success was a mirage. My coworkers made it look easy. I remember how, one day, my colleagues were going to lunch and they asked me if I wanted to join them. I knew I had a lot of ground to make up in a short period of time if I wanted to compete with their experience. I politely declined and stayed behind to get some extra dials in. I remember getting a phone book and starting at *Z* and working my way back to *A*. I figured everyone would have burned up the front of the phone book, so I decided to call people that probably hadn't been touched. I still couldn't put my finger on why I was coming up short. When I assessed my own ability, technically, I checked every box. I even displayed flashes of soft skill mastery. Nevertheless, getting them to sign the agreement was still a herculean exercise. A month had gone by, and I had made a grand total of zero dollars and no cents.

I remember telling my boss, "Something is wrong. It's been a month, and I haven't made any money." He looked me up and down, paused for a second, and then said something I've never forgotten, "They're not buying from you because you don't look like them." My little hand-me-down houndstooth suit was no match for the lion's den I was trying to survive. Like a good manager, he gave it to me straight because he cared. He continued to spit game, "They're coming in here in dirty jeans and work boots, and you're wearing a suit. They think you have no idea about what they do, so why would they buy from you?" Wait, what about dress for success? Jeans? I learned when you go to work, you should look your best. Dress for the position you want, not the position you have, right? Wearing a suit is the baseline to earning professional respect. Little did I know that these contractors were leaving the office doing everything but respecting me. When I thought about what my manager was telling me, I imagined the contractors walking away feeling like I thought I was better than them. Who was I to tell them what they needed when my fingernails were clean, my hands looked like they'd never touched a brick, and my attire resembled that of an entry-level Wall Street intern? They were probably laughing their heads off. No problem. All I needed was the rules. Once I got a full understanding of those, the playing field was immediately leveled.

The next day was a made for TV moment. I came to the office in jeans, sneakers, and a white polo. I went through my normal routine over the phone, got my prospect to agree to coming into the office, and closed my first sale. After that, it was wash, rinse, repeat. Soon I was the number one salesperson in the office. The president of the company was so impressed that he made a visit just to let me know he wanted to open another market and wanted me to spearhead the new operation. He pointed to a map of the country and asked, "So! Where do you want to go?" That's when I learned that dressing for success means becoming their friend. When you dress like their foe, you stay broke.

During that first thirty days when I closed no sales, it had nothing to do with my knowledge. I had done the work to learn the language and understand the nuances. It had nothing to do with my race, religion, or gender. It had nothing to do with my work ethic. I demonstrated I was willing to go the extra mile. It had everything to do with what I was wearing. As I mentioned, before I could utter a word, my appearance was saying things inconsistent with my objective. It was communicating a message with my audience without me having a say in the conversation. It's as if the ventriloquist and the puppet switched roles. Sure, I would have liked the opportunity to control the conversation, but my attire started talking before I could open my mouth. My billboard was advertising a product my audience was not interested in. Ultimately, the filter I gave them to look at me through removed all the positive attributes about my ability to meet their needs as a competent salesperson. The result was a delayed paycheck. The lesson I learned here was that residential contractors are not impressed with fancy suits. I may as well have shown up dressed like a clown because that's how they were looking at me. I lost my audience, and as result, I lost time and money—neither of which I could get back.

WISDOM

Appearance is key in being successful. How do you approach looking the part when conducting yourself in professional circles?

I wanted to know if I was trippin'. We all live in a bubble to a certain extent, and I was curious to find out if my perspective was shared by anyone else. How do you dress for success? The answer seemed to be more gray than black-or-white. What I mean is, there was no one-size-fits-all answer to this question. Yet after presenting this question to each of the people I talked to, it was funny to see how different people arrived at the same conclusion. Turns out I wasn't tripping after all. It can all be summed up with something Veronica said during our conversation: "I strive to understand the environment I'm stepping into before I even get into the room."

I'll start with Stephen and Lesia Linton. I met with this husband-and-wife tandem in their Northwest Houston home on a Sunday afternoon. They approached this from opposite ends of the spectrum, but at the heart of what they were saying was a common underlying piece of wisdom that guides them both to the same outcome. It's interesting that their methods were as calculated as their educational pedigree suggests. She, a Prairie View A&M graduate with a bachelor's degree in chemical engineering; he a University of Texas graduate with a bachelor's in biology. The reason for the dichotomy in their approach has everything to do with the environments they work in. Lesia's professional track includes stops at Accenture, PricewaterhouseCoopers, Shell, Chevron, and Halliburton. And currently, she serves as senior IT organizational change manager at TechnipFMC. Her world is boardrooms, conferences, cubicles, corner offices, and executives. She's very tuned into her audience and what moves them to action. The way she navigates her space is to dress above the norm. Simply put, if the expectation is that employees should dress business casual, then she goes one step beyond and dresses in business attire. Her experience is that people equate competency with looks. In addition to that, her petite stature is perceived as youthfulness and, unfortunately, causes her not to be taken seriously. In order for her to be considered a worthy member of respected professionals, she can't afford to blend in with the majority of the working population. It's as if she uses her attire to make her two feet taller. Despite her unassuming size, she's able to command a level of respect that most women would love to have in a business environment. With an acute sense of what her audience responds to in the workplace, she's able to solicit the response she wants.

Stephen, her husband, is a successful sales professional and entrepreneur. This is one of the smartest bruthas I know. His book smarts rival his hood knowledge, and his hood knowledge is just as valuable as his book smarts. This man has dropped so much wisdom on me I feel like he's Morpheus and I'm Neo. In his twenty-year tenure with a worldwide financial services and communications company, there was only one way for him to govern himself with regards to dressing the part. Unlike his wife, it wasn't with a suit. When I asked him this question, without hesitation he looked at me and said in a matter-of-fact way, "I cater to the demographic." For him, there was no other way to operate if he were to be successful. In essence, that's the same answer as Lesia. "In my line of work, I deal with blue-collar people and sometimes no-collar people. My audience is the unbanked. They live in the hood. I can't go G'd up or I'd lose my audience. What's worse, I'd make myself a mark." For those of you unschooled in hoodology, that means he would become a target to get robbed...or worse. For Stephen, khakis and a polo were as dressed up as it got. Anything more than that and he'd stand out like a sore thumb—much like I did with my houndstooth suit. That's why he's Morpheus. It didn't take him a month to figure it out. Like Lesia, Stephen manipulates his attire to dictate the response he gets from the people he works with. Like I said, two different ways to get the same point. Understand the environment and the expectations of the audience then make the necessary adjustments to become their friend and not their foe.

The wisdom kept flowing in that direction. Stephen and Lesia weren't the only ones who knew how to make their attire work for them. Summer McElroy, an attorney friend of mine who I'll tell you more about later, mentioned that when you first start out on your professional journey, you have to look like something that makes people comfortable—otherwise they won't want to work with you. Darryl echoed the same thing when he told me that you're charged with making yourself palatable for others. He goes on to say that it's necessary to be the least-threatening version of yourself but the strongest version of yourself at the same time. If not, you run the risk of people turning themselves off to you. Alexandra McCauley, a Keller Williams realtor who works with high net-worth clients in the Greater Houston area, was very clear when she told me that in her line of work, if a client feels you're overdressing, you run the risk of not being trusted. It comes across as fake and diminishes authenticity. With that in mind, business casual is her baseline. Her clientele rarely, if ever, come suited and booted; so she's mindful not to cross that line of looking traditionally professional. To that point, Courtney Elveston agrees with Alexandra. "You have to know your audience. People will welcome you easier if you look the part. Going overboard can come across as intimidating," she says. A few others I spoke with felt the same way about this concept of appealing to the audience.

Byrena understood this as she made the transition from the culinary side of P. F. Chang's to the operational side of the house. In the kitchen, she was known as Chef B. Once she was promoted to the partner role, her environment changed and so did her audience. When that happened, not only did she change up her look but she also asked to be called by her first name. She understood this would allow her to become more personable with patrons as opposed to the normal protocol in the kitchen. It's easier to deescalate situations on the floor when people feel they're talking to a person and not a title. In order to lower the first wall of defense, Byrena dresses like who she wants to connect with. That meant retiring the chef's coat in exchange for slacks and a nice button-down collar shirt. Tyra put it best when she said, "People approach you in certain ways based on how you appear." She says that your professional attire is your armor and your costume. Like an actor/actress, it should remind you that you're *on* and it's time to perform.

Another of my former colleagues who works for a Fortune Global 500 company spoke about accessing the situation she's going into well in advance so she can plan her dress accordingly. Every stage has a different costume. For her, she wants to know if it's a business meeting, will she be with a client, will there be any key stakeholders there, or is this a new relationship? She gives each of those a different look as if to dictate a certain tone.

This is a perfect time for a PSA of my own. Ladies, stop showing all your breast meat at work! Yep, I said it because obviously there are still some of you disrespecting the game. That low-cut blouse or camisole is cool and all for the club or a night out on the town with your friends, but Monday through Friday when we're at work, keep your *girls* covered up. You know your body; you know how your clothes fit; you look in the mirror, and you see it before you leave the house. It's not professional; and honestly, it works against you more than it works for you. A couple people cosigned on this point. One of them being Veronica who told me that you don't want to let your clothes be a distraction; you shouldn't draw too much (of the wrong) attention to yourself. "You want to make sure your look doesn't negatively impact the quality of work you're going to produce," she says. Another of my former colleagues said it's never a good idea to draw too much attention to yourself physically; you should want more attention on the content of your conversation and the quality of your work more than your physical attractiveness. I'll end my public service announcement with this: show me a female executive, CEO, or board member that parades around the office with her breast bubbling out of her blouse, and I'll show you someone that's overcompensating for a shortfall. To Tyra's point, pay attention to the leaders around you and mimic how they dress.

The best anecdote was from Sarah. She told me when she gets dressed, she wants to look strong and not fussy. She had me ROFLOL when she told me about her *concealed weapons.* Like a lot of industries, oil and gas is male dominated. This makes it necessary for a woman to make her presence known. Talk about armor! Sometimes Sarah is faced with addressing a table that may not appreciate the strength that's sitting there with them. When that happens, she'll remove her blazer to show her biceps because she stays in good shape—as you would imagine from a former Marine. When I asked her if there was a subliminal message, she emphatically replied, "Absolutely! I'm strong, so don't mess with me. I'm here to engage." Steven Coleman sums this whole thing up when he says that your conversation and appearance have to match; otherwise, people won't take you seriously. That brings me to a story Charles Epps told me.

A University of Houston graduate with a bachelor of science in industrial engineering, Charles is someone who epitomizes Corporate Swagger. There's "Charles" the project manager who has led both international and domestic teams on major corporate initiatives. I've had the chance to admire his *corporate* side when I visited him in his office as an assistant general manager at Carter's / OshKosh B'gosh. It took me a moment to recognize the transformation he had successfully made since the two of us walked the yard years ago. Then there's "Chuck" who he brings out when he's running his successful photography business. The entrepreneur in him demands that his charm and confidence is on full display when he's in that mode of business. We both attended college together at UT, and ultimately, we ended up pledging the same fraternity. That said, we've shared the same stage performing at step shows, so I've witnessed his *swagger* firsthand as well. He points to one pivotal moment that served as the bedrock for bringing those two personalities together.

Charles recalls a time in his first role straight out of college as a project manager for Carter's. He admits to staying inside his lane and not veering too far from his unique style: jeans, button-down shirt with the front part of the shirt tucked in and tail end of the shirt untucked, sleeves rolled up, and nice shoes. One of his functions was to do financial reporting for the company and send the findings to his manager first thing in the morning in time for a daily meeting. This meeting was for VPs and managers only—not project managers. This meant his manager was the only one on the call to give an account for their area. Often, the manager would come from these meetings asking Charles for further clarification on certain talking points. This stemmed from unanswered questions that were asked during the meeting by senior management. Because his manager wasn't privy to the thought behind Charles' reports, his only response during these meetings was "Let me get back to you." Noticing that there was a gap in communication and that it was causing an appearance of incompetency, Charles told his manager that he needed to be in the room to address any concerns about the work he was responsible for. His manager agreed that it would help clear up some of the questions being asked but also stated that they had never done that because the meeting was for management only. Charles' reply to that was "Well, we're going to start. There are some things I know that you don't, and I need to be in there to answer any questions that come up about the work I'm doing. Right now, when there are questions, you're not able to speak to them. It makes it seem like there's a concern when there really isn't. My part is looking bad, and I want to have a chance to defend my work."

A couple of weeks later, Charles was in that same meeting with the other VPs and managers, and he remained a participant in those meetings from that day forward. Nice story, but what does that have to do with dressing the part? He also told me it was the first and last time he went in there with jeans, a half-tucked shirt, and rolled-up sleeves. He realized he was in the room with the big boys and that no one would take him seriously looking the way he did. I love how he concluded his story. He said, "People on the floor who made $8–$10/hour loved me because the way I dressed fit their mold. People who made $150/hour looked at me and probably thought, *He's not ready*." Charles knew he wanted to make moves and be respected, so he made the adjustments. He understood the business he was in and took a look at people who were at the top. He knew he'd be accepted as part of their fold if he altered his appearance. After that awakening, he worked to find a middle ground between his personal style and how a GM or director should look. I'll leave you with this last nugget of wisdom from Joseph. "Know your culture and know your environment. Know how you want to be perceived. Understand that everyone has a different uniform. Figure out where you want to be in that company, and decide if you want to wear that uniform."

FACT

As much as everyone would like to deny what I'm about to say, the ugly truth is we all participate in judging people by their appearance. This alone doesn't make us bad people. We run the risk of that when we allow that judgment to evolve into poisonous thought patterns that control our behavior toward a given group. There's a defense mechanism that's woven into the fabric of our psyche. I'm talking about the "fight or flight" response. Walter Bradford was the first to describe this theory. He stated that when animals sensed a possible threat, their nervous system would trigger a response preparing them to either fight or flee. Humans are not exempt from this phenomenon. Our very survival from prehistoric times until present day has depended on the successful use of this defense mechanism. So what does that have to do with the corporate environment?

First, consider the fact that if our nervous system is the trigger for this response, then our eyes are the finger that pulls the trigger. Simply put, what we see with our eyes determines how we'll respond. The split-second decision to fight or flee is assisted by identifying how someone looks. Often, this judgment is made based on the outer garments we see others wearing. Fact: the first thing we pay attention to when observing people is usually what they're wearing. Let's give this some historical context. We'll call it tribal garb. Imagine two people of different tribes approaching one another. The speed at which one can determine what they see could be the difference between life or death. On one hand the thought could be, *Oh, you're wearing similar tribal garb as me, so I'm safe.* With this assumption, we could conclude several things: We probably share similar experiences. There's a good chance we know the same people. Chances are we could even talk about the same topics. All of this signifies unity. As a result, walls come down and the invitation to commune can be extended. The welcome sign is turned on and shining brightly. On the other hand, if they had seen someone in the distance wearing the tribal garb from an opposing tribe, mentally, the defense mechanism would kick in. This time the thought could very well be, *Uh-oh, you're wearing a different tribal garb than me. I may need to defend myself. Better yet, I may need to flee.* In each of these situations, one is tasked with retrieving enough visual clues to conclude if they need to engage or disengage with the individual(s) in question. It's a judgmental mind-set that kept people alive.

Centuries later, we still operate under the same premise. Need proof? Try walking through the hood (notice I didn't say *neighborhood*—there's a difference) with the wrong colors on and see what happens. No hood skills? No problem. Show up on a college campus wearing their rival college's jersey or T-shirt. I'm pretty sure in both scenarios you're guaranteed to catch some dirty looks—at minimum. These looks are translated to actions that tell the unwanted person they're not welcome and they won't be accepted.

The same can be said for the business environment. We take one look at the person passing us in the office building, and based on their appearance, we draw a conclusion that triggers our "fight or flight" response. If they're not suited up like us, we assume they're not as important and, thus, wouldn't be welcomed in our professional circles. The opposite is true as well. If the person isn't dressed casual like us, we assume their suit makes them rigid and boring to be around. They surely wouldn't fit in with your easygoing business-casual colleagues. Ponder if you will the comparison between work attire of Wall Street versus that of Silicon Valley. The former is accepted upon sight by members of similar professions if they're dressed in the typical blazer or suit jacket, button-down shirt, suit pants, a tie and dress shoes for men and a skirt or pants suit with heels for women. The latter will easily be identified by their jeans, T-shirt, and casual shoes. Try showing up at Google in a suit and tie, and you'll stick out like that woman in the Matrix with the red dress. Likewise, try showing up for a regular day's work at Goldman Sachs in jeans, a T-shirt, and flip-flops. You already know—you'll get shown the door. That's right, it wouldn't work. Fact: certain environments have a specific protocol when it comes to attire. Fall outside of those lines, and you risk sending a message that says you don't belong.

If you take nothing else away from this chapter, know this: Dressing for success is not just about looking nice in fine clothing. Dressing for success is all about breaching the first layer of your audience's defense, getting through their first filter of assumptions. We'll discuss the other filters in chapters 3 and 4. Your objective is to connect. Your aim is to disarm. Your goal is to persuade. Connect with your audience by way of your appearance. Only after a successful connection is made will you be welcomed in. Disarm their natural defense mechanism by displaying similarities. When their guard is down, you increase your chances of getting closer. Finally, persuade them without saying a word. Since your appearance speaks well before you have an opportunity to open your mouth, make sure your attire is magnetic and draws them in. If you do this, you will have succeeded in becoming their friend and not their foe.

CHAPTER 3

. . . .

Rush Hour Effect

"Do you understand the words that are coming out of my mouth?"

—Chris Tucker as
James Carter in *Rush Hour*

I remember an episode of the *Wile E. Coyote and the Road Runner Show* when the Coyote finally caught the Road Runner. All the times he had fallen of a cliff, gotten blown up, or seen his mastermind plan fail was finally worth it. There he was with the Road Runner in his grasp with no way of escape. Dinner was about to be served, and the Coyote had the only seat at the table. Then it happened. The Coyote looked at the TV screen, paused for a brief second as to make sure he had every viewer's undivided attention, then as a confused look glossed over his face, a thought bubble appeared over his head that asked, "Now what?" ☹ HUH? All that work to catch this thing, and now you don't know what to do with him now that you've caught him? In like fashion, what you've learned thus far is enough for you to level up in your corporate game. Let's say you do the work to get your mind right and you pay attention to your audience to make friends, not foes. You still need to know what to do next. Otherwise, you'd end up in the same place as our animated friend asking "Now what?" As much as it might be a funny sight, I'd be doing you a terrible disservice if I sent you out with just that.

Remember, passing the eyeball test by looking the part only breaches the first layer of your audience's defense. There's still work to be done if you want to achieve Corporate Swagger. How do you take that next step? In order to get even closer to your identified group, you must speak their language. You can only speak their language if you know what they know and share a similar level of comprehension for the things that are common knowledge to them. This step in the process demands a near lifestyle change in your "eating" habits. But I'm not talking about edible food. I'm talking about mental food. You'll need to change what you're feeding your eyes and ears, which will ultimately impact what comes out of your mouth. Do this right, and you will have convinced your audience that you not only belong because you look like them, but they'll also believe you belong because you think like them—talk about a Jedi mind trick. This can only be achieved, young Skywalker, if you commit to becoming a voracious consumer of information. You must find ways to take in knowledge in all forms—television, podcasts, print, and anything else you can find that will add value to what you know. Like a hungry wild animal searching for its next meal, you must crave information and devour it with a hunger that keeps you mentally ready for your next encounter. Sometimes procuring this information means engaging in innovative tactics.

Consider my man Joey Tribbiani. Anyone who knows me on a personal level knows I have a deep affinity for the TV series *Friends*. It's so bad that when I'm traveling on business, I choose my hotel based on their channel lineup. If their cable TV offering doesn't carry the channel I need to watch Rachel, Monica, Phoebe, Chandler, Joey, and Ross…not getting my business. I'm serious. Don't judge me. You have your quirks too.

In season 4, episode 3, Joey is interrupted in the middle of the day by a door-to-door encyclopedia salesman. For as many relationships as his character is known for having, he's not at all known for having them with books. You see, Joey doesn't read much. As a result, there's a void created that yearns to be filled with the necessary information that will bring him up to par with his friends. Due to his lack of intellectual depth, he's limited to appearing like he understands while his other friends fire off banter laced with educational under-tones. If he were able to contribute to the conversations they have in his presence, he would feel like he truly belonged and that he, too, could add value to the seemingly difficult subject matter his friends were discussing. He'd even be able to laugh at the jokes that often went over his head. Without that knowledge, he was left to feel like the third wheel on a date—tolerated out of pity. My bad. Are you that person? If so, you know the feeling.

Back to this episode. The salesman asks *Joey,* "Do your friends ever have a conversation and you just nod along even though you're not really sure what they're talking about?" The befuddled look on Joey's face is all the salesman needs to close the deal. Joey ends up buying *one* encyclopedia because that's all he could afford. Armed now with an array of subjects that all start with the letter *V*, he's ready to engage. That feeling of belonging is all but inevitable. At this point, there's no area where he'll feel left out—except for areas that begin with the other twenty-five letters in the alphabet. At least he'd done his part to come up with a creative solution to solve his prob-lem. To prove as much, he started flexing some of his newly devel-oped muscle by striking up conversations spanning from volcanoes to vivisections. If you know Joey, this doesn't surprise you.

Although portrayed in a fictitious light, the scenario is quite real. It's a classic case of "Ihavenoideawhatyouaretalkingaboutbuti mgoingtoactlikeidoandhopeyouneverfindout-itus." Symptoms are frantic nodding of the head, disingenuous laughter, and occasional embarrassment in group settings. The source of this condition stems from severe knowledge deprivation and the inability to swim in deep intellectual waters. There have been several instances where I've noticed others suffer from the same condition. In full transparency, I'm not immune. I've dealt with this sickness enough times to cause me to find a cure.

EXPERIENCE

I distinctly recall the moment I embarked on my own lifestyle change. My professional world is white collar—no pun intended.

People in the financial industry pride themselves on how smart they are. It's what separates the upper echelon of advisors from the pretenders. Not only that but this intellectual showcase is also always on display—even in places or situations you wouldn't expect. I knew if I wanted to be multifaceted with my people skills and relate to a wider audience, I needed to broaden my means to connect. This meant adjusting my diet. I began to listen to the "language" being spoken around me. In doing so, I was introduced to something known as the "smart comedy" genre. That's when I formed yet another guilty pleasure for Jerry, Elaine, George, and Kramer. 😠 Stop laughing! Let's face it, the predominant audience in my profession isn't watching *Martin*. That's not to say they're all *Seinfeld* fans. From my experience, if those were two points on opposite ends of the spectrum, the vast majority of people I was surrounded by in my profession would relate more to *Seinfeld* references anyway. Few, if any, would have any idea of who Bruh Man was or what floor he lived on. For those of you scratching your heads, he was a character on the sitcom, *Martin*.

I remember watching an episode of my newfound TV show, and as in most sitcoms, the punch line was delivered with the predictable smattering of laughter from the studio audience. The problem was I wasn't laughing. I remember sitting there asking myself, "What just happened? What did I miss?" My first step was to use one of the most valuable lessons I learned in grade-school English class—context clues. That got me close, but that wasn't good enough. I wanted to go as deep as I could to understand the basis for this new type of casual conversation. My next solution was to rewind the television (thank you, Anthony Wood) to see if I had missed a key word, phrase, or crucial plot point I didn't hear initially. Shouldn't have done that. If missing the joke the first time was bad, then missing it the second time when I knew it was coming had me feeling just like…Joey. Not only did a strong sense of mental inadequacy fall on me like Dr. Strange's cloak but now I also felt left out. I kept thinking, 😔 *I want to laugh!*

As bad as that feeling was in the seclusion of my own home, I knew I never wanted to have that feeling in public. When neither of those worked, I devised a more strategic plan for interpreting this foreign "language." Whenever there was a reference made to something I was unfamiliar with, I paused the TV and put my phone/tablet/computer (whatever I had next to me at the time) to good use. I'd look up the focal point of the punch line and read everything I needed to read on that topic until I developed a fluency in that area of discussion. Like a regimented athlete, I committed to getting as many repetitions as I could. I watched that show any time it was on TV. After all, this was a nonnegotiable if I wanted to gain the trust of varying audiences.

Once I realized I had a process that worked, I expanded what I watched from sitcoms to world news. I was especially intrigued by the one-on-one interviews with prominent figureheads. I would watch them and imagine myself in the seat being interviewed. I'd play this game with myself to see if I completely understood the questions being asked and attempt to answer them myself. Then I would switch roles and imagine being the interviewer. I would attempt to fashion a question based on the person's previous response. Soon I found myself thinking like the interviewer and asking the same questions, making the same points. Once fluent in that space, I transitioned to books, newspapers, magazines. I became a voracious consumer of information.

It's probably not as cerebral as you anticipated. One might even argue the validity of my process. You may be surprised to know that what I did was no different from what someone from a foreign country does when they come to America. I've had several friends and colleagues tell me that they learned English by watching certain shows on television. None of the shows would you label as educational. You know what though? Those people are 100 percent fluent and proud of their unconventional learning process. They, too, had a Joey moment.

All I did was submerge myself into a world I was unfamiliar with. Now I consider myself "multilingual" in a sense. As a result, I can communicate to varying degrees of audiences. From those that speak *Martin* to those fluent in *Seinfeld,* janitors or CEOs, Main Street or Wall Street, hood or the burbs. Whatever the situation, I've equipped myself to breach the second layer of acceptance. You can too. Like Joey, sure, my process was unconventional, but also like him, at least I was smart enough to admit to a deficiency and seek creative measures to overcome it. I don't want to overstate the methodology of overcoming this challenge and imply that watching TV sitcoms will get you promoted or land you that big account. I do want to impress upon you the importance of developing a way to become multifaceted in your communication abilities. Find a way to consume information from a variety of perspectives. It does no good to look like you belong at the party if when you get there, you can't contribute to the conversation.

Another experience happened only a few years ago. The funny thing is that it involved me spending money on a resource that would, in the end, prove to be the link between me and my audience. No, I wasn't interrupted in the middle of the day by a door-to-door encyclopedia salesman. However, I did obtain a limitless supply of conversation material as a result of the purchase. Since I've been licensed in the financial industry, I've always been surrounded by people that had at least a decade or more experience than I had. That being the case, I had to work extra hard to prove that this college dropout who majored in vocal performance belonged in the industry—that I had what it took to be successful. Thank God for my wife.

Enna has always had my back. I am what I am because of God's grace and my wife's support. She knew my plight and, in silence, decided to provide a solution. One morning I went outside and there was a newspaper at the front door. This wasn't just any newspaper. In my eyes, this was *the* newspaper. This was the newspaper (in my opinion) that defined *business savvy*. I pulled the plastic back, and yep, there it was the *Wall Street Journal*. My wife had secretly purchased a subscription for me so I could break the professional language barrier. To me this was the gold standard of all business resources and the basis for the type of casual conversations I wanted to be a part of. I had always marveled at people who knew how to seamlessly insert a *WSJ* headline into their conversations to validate their point. All this time I had been left in the dark, and it was all my fault. I hadn't done the work to become multilingual in *Wall Street*

Journal-ese, *Forbes*-ish, or *Bloomberg*-an. But thanks to my wife, I was officially enrolled, and my textbook had arrived. Class was in session.

Morning after morning, I read each edition of my new "textbook" from the banner headline to the final sentence on the back page. Most of the time it was tedious, intimidating, and even embarrassing. I understood a disproportionate amount of information. None of that mattered. I planned on downloading this information into my human operating system in anticipation that one day I'd could upload it onto someone else's hard drive. I continued to consume the information hoping that one day I'd be able to use it for the benefit of infiltrating (even further) this group of professionals—proving that I was to be taken seriously in this industry.

Months went by, and what was once tedious became interesting and what was intimidating became inviting; my embarrassment was replaced with confidence. The only problem was I had neglected my reading for a few weeks, and I had several days of unread newspapers underneath my computer desk. I had a stack about twelve inches high, and it got higher as the days went by. I was determined to catch up, so I committed to read them during any downtime I had. Little did I know my procrastination would prove to be beneficial. I was consuming so much at a consistent pace that it was coming out of my pores. I was talking about articles at dinner. I'd see something on television and tell my wife, "I was just reading about that!" She had created a monster. However, I was still in waiting for that golden opportunity to put my knowledge to work.

Like any class, there's always a test to prove you've mastered the course. My test came one morning when I was meeting my district manager and one of my financial advisor colleagues for breakfast. I arrived at the restaurant earlier than everyone else with my *WSJ* in hand as if it were an accessory to my business ensemble. Since I was still in the process of catching up after days of procrastination, I thought I'd make the best use of the time and get some reading in while I waited.

My colleagues finally arrived. From a distance one of them could see that I had a newspaper in front of me. Without hesitation he asks, "Oh, what are you reading there, the sports page?" Inside I'm like "😆 Really? See a brother with a newspaper and it's the sports page?" Outside I'm like "🙂 Actually, I'm reading the *Wall Street Journal*. I got behind on my subscription and decided to use the time to catch up." I rattled off a headline and some supporting facts I had just read. I wanted to emphasize my level of comprehension and possibly eliminate any ideas he may have had that I was just looking at the pictures—just saying. Once he heard me speaking his "language," he immediately began sharing how he, too, had fallen behind on his *WSJ* subscription.

And there we were—the two of us regaling ourselves with tales of world news, politics, economy, tech, and other common sections of the *Journal*. In that moment, we had as much to share with each other as two high school classmates at a class reunion. What happened? How did we get there? I used dialect to my advantage and successfully broached his second layer of defense. His first layer was a layup because we were colleagues. I already looked the part. All I had to do to get even closer to him was convince him that my vocabulary was rooted in the same dictionary as his. Final exam: A+. Even if nothing about me changed in his eyes, even if he meant nothing by the sports page comment, even if he was just saying the first thing that came to mind as he entered the restaurant, from my own perspective, I gained a level of confidence, respect, and credibility. I even gained an ally. All because he understood the words that were coming out of my mouth.

WISDOM

Jargon is critical in flexing your professional prowess. It's like learning a new language that proves you belong. How would you explain the importance of being able to talk the talk?

I always joke with my wife about this. I sarcastically tell her that when it comes to cerebral matters, who am I, right? What do I know? I'm just little Rodney Jones from the neighborhood. I have 274 Twitter followers. By social media standards, I don't even exist. You've got a reason to look at me sideways when I'm spitting knowledge. That's why I love wisdom. I can rely on an echo chamber of

62

credible others to deliver the same message. No ego here. I don't care who you get the message from, I just want you to get it. Like before, there was a resounding undertone in everyone's answers. It was best summarized by Anthony when he told me, "If you don't speak the language, you either get kicked out of the tribe or get relegated to the grunt work." Now that we understand the gravity, let's unpack this a bit more.

I call Summer McElroy to the stand. Summer is a University of Texas undergrad with a bachelor of science in kinesiology and exercise science. She later enrolled at the Thurgood Marshall School of Law at Texas Southern University and graduated with her juris doctor. She now manages her own multiservice law firm that specializes in wealth management. Who better to speak on the importance of talking the talk than someone who makes their living based on how well they communicate on behalf of others? Summer is an expert at changing her communication style to fit her audience. Her clients aren't interested in speaking legalese. In her words, "They don't want to hear that." She explained that her first objective is to earn her client's trust. Summer has a solution, and she needs her client to buy into that solution for their sake. Talking over their heads will work against her. She saves the legal jargon for when she's talking to the opposing lawyer. When engaged in a back-and-forth with her counterpart, her audience and objective changes. Here it's all about gamesmanship. It's a high-stakes chess match where every word carries with it someone else's fate. But then there's a third audience—the judge. When she approaches the bench, Summer needs to elevate her communication to another level beyond when she's sparring with the other lawyers. Here her objective is to justify her tactics and express to the decision-maker why said strategy is necessary for her to make her case. That's when it dawned on me. Her mouthpiece has to be so fluid that she can bounce from the client to the other lawyer to the judge. In most instances, she does this in a matter of seconds. Thanks, Summer, for giving us all a textbook example of how to adjust to our audience on the fly in the midst of pressure situations.

The echo chamber got louder when I asked Byrena Washington this question. You'll remember that she's the chef that worked her way from cook to management in the culinary side of P. F. Chang's then ultimately transitioned to the front of the house where she's now more customer-facing. Her answer, however, had absolutely nothing to do with business, but the premise of what she did remained consistent with what you should do in professional settings.

A while back, before she got married, Byrena had a "friend" she used to hang out with. This young lady had very staunch Catholic parents who did not approve of their daughter's lifestyle. So much to the point that they forbade her from bringing anyone to their home who was gay or lesbian. You know how you used to tell your boyfriend/girlfriend to come by the crib during that window of time when you thought your folks wouldn't be there? Well, that happened with these two. Byrena was invited over, and to her surprise, the dad was posted up outside when she arrived. Obviously, this was not planned. Neither the young lady nor Byrena expected her dad to be there. Too late now. Game on! Remember, appearance is the first layer of the defense mechanism we're tasked with disarming. I like what Joseph Norman says, "If by chance you take an 'L' on the look, you still have a shot. If you can express yourself in a way that shows you can function at the top of that game, you've leapfrogged the competition."

I mention that because Byrena's look was one that this young lady's parents would readily identify as someone living the type of lifestyle they disagreed with. To give you the visual, Byrena is someone that rocks either cornrows, a fade, or some kind of short haircut. Depending on the day, you may catch her in a hat turned backward with some fly kicks. She always has a nice timepiece on that prominently displays both of her fully tatted sleeves. Typically, her and her circle of friends go by some kind of nickname that amplifies a more masculine persona. Imagine her stepping out of a car at this person's home to be greeted by a parent that is vehemently against what's going down. She approaches the father and greets him with a smile followed by a warm salutation filled with respect culminating with her replacing her street name with her full name. Time went by, and the two of them continued their conversation outside. Days later this same young lady told Byrena, "I don't know what you and my dad talked about, but he likes you! He said you are welcomed over to our house anytime and that he wished I had more friends like you." Mic. Drop. Herein was an example of someone who was prejudged based on their appearance and rightly so. We are what we advertise, there's no getting around that. Sarah mentioned that you have to understand the person you're speaking to and adapt to them. Thoma agreed when he told me that a lot of it is determined by who you're talking to. The goal is to remain authentic while simultaneously making your audience feel comfortable. When you look at Byrena's situation, she did just that. She immediately peeped game: assessed her environment, sized up her audience, made the proper adjustments, and delivered her part of the dialogue in a way that allowed her to remain true to who she was but also connect with her audience. It's like Tyra told me: it's important to be able to display this ability because it's how you let your audience know you belong.

In both Summer's and Byrena's situations, there's yet another element that can easily be overlooked—there's a bunch of work that has to be done beforehand. Before experiencing that level of acceptance, first determine your learning platform. Courtney Elveston, who I'll introduce you to later, puts a premium on active listing. Veronica reads a lot to understand different tones of different businessmen and how they see the world. Lesia Linton told me she digs around on the company website/intranet looking for the abbreviation glossary to familiarize herself with the onslaught of three-letter terminology that's guaranteed to show up in any given meeting. I'll leave you with this. My man Steven Coleman put it best when he said, "It takes a lot of self-development. You have to commit yourself to lifelong learning. Whether it's technical, formal, informal, school of hard knocks, ear hustlin', or old-school hustlin', you have to take what you learn in those areas and master the conversation." He went on to say that learning is how you build the content of your conversation library. This way you can pull from previous lessons and carry on a conversation with any audience. Bottom line: it doesn't happen without putting in the effort.

FACT

Language does many things. In the context of this book and the concepts I'm sharing with you, I want to focus on three facts about language that are relevant in our professional life as well as our personal lives. One, language identifies who we are. Two, language separates us. Three, language unites us. I need to shine a light on these truths so that you understand the game you're playing. Few people will be bold enough to admit any of these facts out loud. This is why you have this book in your hands—to learn what isn't being openly shared.

Language identifies who we are. In February of 2017, Pew Research Center did a study on how people define national identity. They surveyed people from fourteen different countries. The majority of people in each of those countries agreed that their primary determining factor for considering if someone was a true member of that nation depended on the native language they spoke. For instance, 70 percent of Americans say it's important to them for someone to be able to speak English. In their eyes, this was a justifiable reason to be considered American. An overwhelming 80 percent of Dutch, British, Hungarians, and Germans believe the ability to converse in their country's language is very important to nationality.

Let's take a step back from being so academic and look at this in a practical sense. We're talking about how language can define who we are. Consider these two phrases:

- I'm out here trying to make this paper so I can set the fam up on that George and Weezie. N'yamean?
- I'm working hard trying to earn a living so I can provide a comfortable lifestyle for my family. You can appreciate that, right?

Both phrases mean the same thing. If you're honest with yourself, when you read the first one, you probably identified it with someone from the hood or someone younger, maybe even someone less educated. When you read the second phrase, you probably identified it with someone more corporate, refined, educated, and probably even upstanding. I'm not bashing either way. I'm just spittin' facts. If this is the game, we need to know the rules. Fact: judgment of who you are is often made based on the "language" you speak. That same judgment will either be your ticket in or what keeps you out.

Language separates us. There's no more effective way to exclude someone than by speaking a language they can't understand. This isn't anything new. You've felt it before. If not, you've seen it happen to others. One moment everyone in a group is speaking English. Then suddenly those in the group that share a second language break off into a conversation in their native tongue. This leaves anyone that doesn't share that ability to communicate in a different language standing on the sidelines with that "What'd they say?" look on their face. Boom! Separation achieved.

One morning during my quiet time, I came across this text in one of the books I use as a reference that brings this fact to life:

> We imagine language was invented so we might communicate with each other better.
>
> Maybe not.
>
> Language is oft about exclusion—across an ethnic border where we speak differently or across borders, we build intentionally, to separate and divide. In language we keep others out. We can only be decoded or deciphered by one who speaks our language, by one who speaks us.
>
> Across class or geography, across disciplines like medicine or economics, jargon and acronyms are given to separate us from those who must never grasp what we have taken years to learn. Human beings love not to be understood.

Babble.

Babel.

A confusion of tongues.

These were the words of Paul David Hewson in his foreword in *The Message 100: The Story of God in Sequence—a bible*. Would you like it better if I told you that Paul's stage name is Bono? Yeah, that one. The lead singer for U2. Did you catch what I did there? I purposefully separated my audience using language. I used his formal name to bring a sense of sophisticated value to the reference. Then I used his stage name to speak to those of you that honor his entertainment street cred. Two different audiences separated by language. If it can happen by manipulating the words on a page, how much more do you think it's happening in business?

It's a double-edged sword. We learn a language to be included; at the same time, we exclude those that don't know the language. We even wear it as a badge of honor. "I speak four languages." That's great and admirable and impressive. It also speaks of a proficiency to separate. Again, I'm not bashing. These are just facts. This is what language does. It serves and severs, builds and breaks, connects and...I couldn't find the right word that started with *c*, so I'll just say *disconnects*.

Language unites us. You've heard people use the phrase, "Now you're speaking my language." This is an expression of union, oneness, and agreement. There's a level of connectivity that's achieved when we're speaking the same language—both figuratively and literally. One of the strongest pillars of a relationship is communication. I was watching an episode of *Married at First Sight* with my wife, and there was a young couple that ended up getting a divorce after spending eight weeks together. This show is a dose of reality TV mixed with social experimentation. Two people agree to an arranged marriage with a complete stranger where the first time they meet is at the altar. At the end of the experiment, they decide if they want to stay married or get divorced. This couple decided to part ways because they both had different definitions of gender roles. In that subject of the relationship, they did not speak the same language. Ultimately, this proved to be a challenge for them, which led to divorce. The opposite is fact as well. For couples that have healthy relationships, they typically speak the same language. Gender roles mean the same thing for both; *clean* means the same for both; *love* means the same thing for both people. When you speak the same language, unity is inevitable.

The benefit is quite clear. What's at stake for you is a higher level of confidence, credibility, and respect. Imagine what would happen to your success meter if you were able to erase communication barriers. However, to get there takes work. Just like learning any language, you must commit to the process. It's going to take time, and you may even get behind. Don't let that stop you from continuing to take steps forward. Find the tactic that works for you—TV shows that open your mind to a different perspective, subscriptions to magazines or newspapers, podcasts, books, whatever works. Become a voracious consumer of information. When you're ready, the opportunity will present itself. As the poem by Rudyard Kipling goes, 'If you can talk with crowds and keep your virtue, or walk with kings—nor lose the common touch..." When you prove that you can connect to diverse audiences and fit in on a level that tells them you belong, you're one step closer to Corporate Swagger.

CHAPTER 4

· ·

Take a Bow

"If you stay ready, you ain't gotta get ready."
—Suga Free, 1997

You've taken in quite a bit, and there's more to come. Before we go on, let's take inventory of where you should be in your progress:

- Your mental toughness is steadily approaching a ten, so you're winning the battle of you vs. you.
- You've taken the steps to remove any premature barriers by catering to the optics of your audience. You're making friends, not foes.
- Next, you studied their dialect to make sure you could speak the language.

This will get you noticed and invited to the party. You'll even be able to get past security because you know the password. What happens when you walk through the door? This is when the game gets real and it's time to prove you belong at the party. If you can't convince them that you belong by giving them a stellar performance, you'll never be invited back. It's lights, camera, action—you're on. This is when we cure any lingering symptoms of the imposter syndrome. You may feel like a fish out of water, but I got you covered.

Ever heard the phrase "That's like putting lipstick on a pig"? If not, let me school you. It's an expression that means regardless of the effort you go through to make the exterior look good—makeup, weave, Botox, clothes, or any other outward changes—the true nature of the person will eventually reveal itself. Dress it up all you want. It's still a pig. Now, no one wants to be compared to an animal and I'm sure, least of all, a pig. There are other phrases that are just as popular that convey the same message: *studio gangsta* refers to a rapper that makes songs falsely claiming to live a lifestyle of gang-related activity such as selling drugs, killing people, or anything else illegal; *Instagram famous,* as defined by Urban Dictionary, means not really famous on Instagram because about all your followers are ghost followers, again creating a facade that attempts to get your audience to believe one thing when the opposite is true; *ghetto fabulous* means living a "barely get by" lifestyle while representing outwardly that you can afford the latest fashions and accessories. All these define a person that is operating in a space outside of their natural habitat in efforts to fit in. In order to avoid getting made (having their cover blown) and being exiled from the group, they have to resort to putting lipstick on a pig.

The same principle is found in a situation where a person is attending an elegant gala for the first time. Their goal is to fit in with the rest of the socially elite. The slightest questionable move and game over—they're exposed and left to feel like the outsider they were trying so hard not to be. The defining moment happens when everyone sits down to eat. We've all been on one side of this table or the other. Either you're the person looking across at the individual that has that "Why are there so many forks near my plate?" look on their face or you're the person everyone is watching as you try to figure out why there are so many forks near your plate. We see the same thing play out in the person with the $900 pair of stiletto heels. Yeah, she can afford the shoes, but the graceful walk that should accompany this pair of fine European heels is nowhere to be found. Busted! You're out of your league and everyone knows. It is a beautiful thing when you just so happen to lay eyes on a unicorn—the person that is capable of pulling it off. There's nothing more gratifying than seeing the person that has never been to a gala navigate the dinner-table terrain with ease. Without hesitation, they know which fork to use for their salad and which one to use for dinner. Nothing elicits that subtle head nod of acceptance more than watching a young lady wear a pair of sophisticated shoes like she was walking down a runway in Milan during fashion week. She exudes so much grace that you would never imagine she was from the hood and not the burbs. In both instances, those moments of euphoria don't happen unless some work takes place beforehand. So let's get to work.

There are two components to making this happen. First, you need to act like you've been there before. Consider Barry Sanders. For all the electrifying moves this Hall of Fame running rack had on the field, you wouldn't be able to tell from his demeanor in each of the 109 times he found the end zone during his NFL career. He acted like he had been there before. Scoring a touchdown wasn't new to him. He practiced tirelessly and expected to get to the end zone. When his work produced the desired results, it was no big deal. He had been there before. What was his signature touchdown celebration? A simple underhand toss of the football to the nearest official. He wasn't flamboyant, demonstrative, or boastful. His actions proved that he knew how to conduct himself because he wasn't in foreign territory.

Unfortunately, you can't act like you've been there if you don't do the work. The next component is the age-old favorite: practice. To quote Alan Iverson (if you haven't seen this video, you have to look it up on the internet), "What are we talking about? Practice? We're talking about practice, man. I mean, listen, we're talking about practice, not a game, not a game, not a game, we talking about practice!" Yes. In order to avoid faking it and risking eventual embarrassment, you're going to have to practice.

When you're familiar with someone, something, or even a situation, you begin to develop a level of trust in that person, thing, or situation. Once trust is achieved, you can predict certain outcomes. When the crystal ball is in your hand and you can predict the outcome, there's not too much that will surprise you. When you can mitigate surprises, you increase your control of the situation. Ultimately, you want to be in control of as many situations as possible. Even if you can't control the entire situation you're in, you should still look to control pieces of the situation. When you're in control, you win. It all starts with practice.

I hear you though. Fake it till you make it, right? Wrong! I cringe every time I hear that phrase. I disagree with the "fake it" part. Faking it means pretending to be someone you're not. On the contrary, I don't want you to ever be someone you're not. My intention is to help you integrate who you are to fit any environment. There's a difference here. When you pretend or fake it, you lose yourself. I mentioned this earlier. At your core, you are who you are and that's a wrap! There's no changing that part of you. You can try to fake it, but inevitably the person you were trying to hide will emerge like that one relative at a family function—you can only hide them for so long before they find their way to the front where they embarrass the entire family. Yep, that'll be you embarrassing yourself and everyone around you once your lipstick wears off. Faking it until you make it is contrary to what Corporate Swagger is all about. This is how you avoid faking it. This is how you prove to your audience that you belong. Let them see that you know how to conduct yourself in certain environments because you've put in the reps during practice. That goes for practicing to eat at a gala, practicing walking in expensive heels, practicing a particular talking point for an upcoming conversation. It doesn't matter. This isn't about setting you up for failure by being someone you're not. You don't need to read a book on how to embarrass yourself. This chapter is about showing you how to bypass the next level of defense so that you prove you belong.

EXPERIENCE

When I moved to Houston, Texas, I quickly became enamored with the Galleria Mall. This mall is prominently located in the Uptown District. Its surrounded by high-rise condominiums, beautiful office buildings, luxury hotels, and signature eateries. I had never been in such an upscale shopping area like this before. Your hometown mall may be better, but for me, seeing four floors of iconic stores I had only seen on television or heard mentioned in song lyrics was jaw-dropping. I remember when I was a child how my mom would prep me before we entered a fancy store—I'm talking about Ché Kmart, Lé Sears, or JC Pennois. She would tell me, "You don't want nothing. You don't need nothing. Don't ask for nothing. Most of all, you bet-not touch nothing." From an early age, this seed produced a mind-set that told me there would always be things too expensive for me to even touch, let alone have as my own. This "if you can't pay for it, don't pick it up" mentality also had me convinced that there are some stores I have no business in entering. You can imagine my childlike awe as I walked by stores like Tiffany, Salvatore Ferragamo, Gucci, Burberry, Louis Vuitton. 😬💬I heard my mom's voice: "You bet-not touch nothing." Year after year I would frequent the Galleria only to find myself accepting the lies that I didn't belong in these ritzy fashion establishments. If I did decide to cross the threshold of one of these places, I would have done so without the confidence, the courage, or the slightest idea of how to conduct myself once inside. Surely the people that shop in Neiman Marcus have a different demeanor than the people that shop at discount department stores. Don't get me wrong. Some of my best gear comes from discount department stores—and I'm proud of it! I only juxtapose the two for the purpose of depicting the difference in mind-set between the two types of the clientele. I knew that if I picked up an item of clothing that shattered my definition of affordable, I would be exposed as someone that could barely afford to breath the boujee air. People would see the pig even though the lipstick was on thick. If I was going to avoid the embarrassment and have that euphoric experience, I had to go to work. Yep, "What are we talking about? Practice? We're talking about practice, man…"

I started by changing my thinking. Soon there was a chain reaction. My words changed. Ultimately, my actions changed, which is what I needed to have happen if I were going to add this facet to my arsenal of blending in. Remember that scene in *Avengers: Infinity War* where Dr. Strange was glitching? Tony Stark asked him what he was doing, and he said, "I went forward in time to view alternate futures, to see all the possible outcomes of the coming conflict." Yeah, that was me. I played out every possible outcome. Like Dr. Strange, all I saw was one option to winning my conflict.

To change my thinking, I first adapted the notion that expensive is relative. What costs a lot to one person may be chump change to another. So I imagined having a different perspective on what expensive meant. Then I asked myself, how would someone that has the money act if they were looking at something and price wasn't a factor? The answer deposited a new entry into my personal vocabulary bank. I imagined they'd say something like, "That's not bad." My thinking was if I don't give any indication that I don't belong, they won't have reason to believe I don't belong. Instead of seeing the $250 necktie and saying something like, "What the crap? Who in their right mind would pay this for a tie?" I would flex my chin muscles, poke out my bottom lip, and calmly respond in a nonchalant way, "That's not bad." Although my inner self would be trippin' on how a necktie could cost as much as a car payment—especially when I was accustomed to spending $9 for a tie. My outer self would demonstrate an unflappable disposition that would tell the salesperson that I belonged there. I practiced this response until it became second nature. I would find myself in grocery stores saying, "That's not bad." I wanted this to be as natural as the call and response that happens in church when the preacher asks for an amen and the congregation answers accordingly. I practiced until it became an ordinary phase— something I said without thinking. You may argue that I was faking it. I would counter your argument by adding that I practiced until I internalized more than the action but the reason behind the action. Expensive *is* relative. If I ever wanted to truly be accepted into circles outside of my league, I had to think like them. This was me adapting a different perspective until it became my own—thus avoiding being fake. I might not have the same resources, but I understood their thinking and that was real.

The day finally came. I walked into the Galleria and headed straight for Nordstrom. I beelined it to the men's section. After casually walking around for a whole minute, like clockwork, a sales associate approached me. I picked up a display shoe that caught my attention. I ran my hands across the fine leather, careful not to turn the shoe over too soon. I didn't want it to seem like price was the first thing on my mind. That would have been a dead giveaway—cover blown. After all, I knew I was being watched. I continued to admire the stitching on the welt of the shoe before moving to inspect the insole for comfort. For dramatic effect, I put the shoe on the floor to catch a view of it just as if I were wearing it. I picked the shoe up and decided this would be the time to ask. "What's the price on this one?" He told me some ridiculous amount that had me doing funny math in my head. Nevertheless, I was ready for this moment. Familiarity = trust = predictability. I flexed the chin, flashed the bottom lip, and confidently said, "That's not bad." Peeping game, he then asked if I wanted to try it on. Uh-oh! I hadn't practiced this much. Was he calling my bluff? Did he know that I'd have to forfeit half of my rent money to buy these shoes? I chose to do what any good performer does—I kept going. I replied, "Sure. Let's see how it feels." Having some time to think while he went to retrieve the shoes, I reminded myself of the process that got me this far—new way of thinking leads to new word choice, which leads to new actions. He wasn't ready for what I was about to hit him with. I had made up my mind that by the time I walked out of that store, he would be calling me a snooty rich bastard behind my back. I tried on the shoes, did a nice pace back and forth to sell it, took them off, and gave them back to the salesperson. He gave me the predictable "Would you like for me to bag those up for you?"

That's when I hit him with "You know, I thought they would feel as good as they looked, but that wasn't the case. Thanks for your help, but no thank you." Like a boss, I walked out...with my rent money and my dignity! I heard a voice in my head as I was walking out. This time it wasn't my mom telling me not to touch anything. It was a different voice telling me to take a bow.

WISDOM

There's talking the talk, and there's walking the walk. How do you get ready for "the show" to ensure you're always giving a stellar performance?

I know you're probably tired of hearing it, but there's no way around it. It reminds me of a post-game interview I saw. Some would argue that he's the GOAT on the hardwood. To me there's only one G.O.A.T., and he made the number 23 famous. That's my Chi-town bias talking. Anyway, this highly skilled three-time NBA Champion, four-time NBA Most Valuable Player, two-time Olympic gold medalist, and two-time high school Mr. Basketball award recipient was wearing a hat that read "There is no magic pill." Compare that statement to the fraction of accolades mentioned, and it almost makes you wonder—if not a pill, maybe a potion, right? Nope! The people I asked this question to could all wear the same hat. They have the accomplishments to back it up, and when you put their collective responses to the fire, they can all be melted down into one of my favorite sayings, "If you stay ready, you ain't gotta get ready."

Before we get into the meat of this, it's appropriate to share a word of caution. This came up in a couple of the conversations I had. It struck a nerve, so I wanted to make sure to pass it along. Courtney Elveston is a former colleague of mine. She graduated from the University of Louisiana at Monroe. Currently, she works as an accountant in a CPA firm. Our paths crossed when we both worked for a prominent talent acquisition agency. What impressed me about Courtney was how she handled herself when it was time to take the stage. Game peeps game; so when we met, I could tell we had something in common when it came to playing this corporate game. That common quality was revealed when I accompanied her on a client visit. Watching her perform validated what she told me during our conversation. Her immediate response to my question was "Once again, it comes down to being genuine." She put a great deal of weight on this prerequisite. Aware that adapting to your environment and your audience is a must, she never relinquishes her hold on who she is. To do so, she says, would communicate the wrong motive and risk the entire production falling apart. What I saw during that client visit was someone that could camouflage their small-town upbringing and blend in with elite C-level executives. This was a common thread both of us had woven into our fabric. In her words, "Sometimes you have to be a chameleon but still have to be genuine." When the chameleon changes color, it's still a lizard. It doesn't turn into a leaf when the situation calls for it to hide. It simply blends in with its surroundings to serve a temporary purpose. The same is true in the workplace and in business. If you've done the work, then blending in becomes natural and no one will be able to tell otherwise.

Tyra Metoyer and Byrena Washington give their best performances while rooted in the same mind-set. Tyra shared with me that it's mandatory that you decide who you are and what you want to be known for because, ultimately, your performance reflects your persona. For instance, Tyra gets stuff done. She wants to be known as a problem solver and solution finder. Those two things are evident in how she approaches the stage of her workplace. When she's done, that's the impression she's left on her audience. But it's easy for her to do because that's who she is all the time. The opposite of this would be what Byrena referred to as the "dog and pony" show. Urban Dictionary defines it as "an elaborate act of bull shirt, generally used to distract attention away from the sheer uselessness of the actual project or act." Couldn't have said it better. She further cautions that this is typically a feeble cry of acceptance. "Sometimes we put all our effort into being valued, included, or received that we'll come across as fake," she says. Not that acceptance is particular to one generation or another, but I found her final thought on this question to be something everyone should be aware of. That is, chasing acceptance exposes a willingness to sacrifice the better part of yourself when you're younger, more impressionable, and eager to be welcomed by a certain group or circle. Once you understand the importance of authenticity, you can move to the root of giving a good performance. It's best summed up in these three words from Joseph Norman, "Competency is cash."

The next area of focus when ensuring a stellar performance has to do with your ability to do what's being expected of you. This is your performance, and your audience has paid a handsome salary, commission, or fee to see you wow them. How do you do this? According to Joseph, performance is about taking the time to become highly competent in whatever you're hired to do. Developing that competency is what gets you longevity. What he's referring to there is staying power. When people appraise your value and it proves to be consistently beneficial, they're more inclined to keep you around. Sometimes they will even create positions/roles for you. Along those same lines, Darryl Blackburn expressed that it goes back to a supreme confidence in your qualifications. Where does this supreme confidence come from? Darryl says if you put in the time, you'll end up knowing more about the things under your umbrella of responsibility than anyone else. When it's game time, you increase your chances for success exponentially.

If you or anyone you know has ever performed live onstage, what Darryl told me next should have your head nodding. He said, "The people that put on the best show are the ones who know their lines and the other person's lines." He's spot on! Actors/actresses at the top of their game not only know their part but they also make an extra effort to go beyond what's expected. They study the lines of their costars as well. Having this degree of proficiency allows them to elevate the overall outcome and compensate for any unforeseen performance blunders. How is that possible? How did they know what the person opposite of them was supposed to say? I like Stephen Linton's answer. He told me that you need to practice performing in your discomfort zone until it becomes your new comfort zone. I hear you though. But, Rodney, that's not my job. That's their responsibility. I shouldn't be expected to do what someone else is supposed to do. Don't tell that to Tyra. Her response to that assertion was "People need to let that go. The whole objective to your career is to build new skills, competencies, and relationships. You may have more work, but so what!" The benefit, Tyra says, is easily overlooked.

Think about it for a second. When you put in the time to build your skill set and sharpen your competencies by functioning outside of your comfort zone, you put yourself in position to be invited into areas that were once closed off. Even if you're asked to sit and observe a meeting or to merely take notes, you've just become the keeper of the golden scrolls. The information is squarely in your hands. Imagine the knowledge you'd have access to that others didn't.

Thoma told me a story that depicts the magnitude of preparation. This, too, happened in a social setting, but again, it's a transferrable principle and can be used in the same manner in professional settings. He started the story by telling me that practice matters. Have you heard that somewhere before? The setting was his brother's birthday party. Family and friends were gathered around the pool celebrating another year. People were singing, laughing, conversing, everything you would do at a pool party. However, Thoma functions under the mentality that the lights are always on, so you always have to be prepared. The way he goes about his preparation is stealth. In his words, "In my mind—among beer, Crown, swimming, and wine—I'm preparing." On the outside, it appears as if he's allowing himself to be just as caught up in the moment as everyone else. On the inside he is going all *Rain Man / Beautiful Mind*. Eventually, he expects the stage to come to him. In efforts not to face-plant, he prepares even as the moment is evolving around him. This wasn't something he spent the previous night toiling over. This was during the festivities. As anticipated, the time came, and Thoma was asked to give a speech. No problem. He knew his value. He understands the environment. Time to give the audience what they wanted—and he did just that. He delivered a heartfelt speech that strummed the heartstrings of everyone listening.

When I asked Steven Coleman this question, he opened me up to a term he uses called personhood. Like you, I had to ask what that was. He shared with me that he knows his value and he also knows his personhood, or what makes him who he is at his core. Another way of looking at it is the things that shape your belief system. His list consisted of the following:

- Experiences
- Relationships
- Knowledge
- Accomplishment
- Education

When you think about the question of how you prepare to give a stellar performance, personhood makes sense. The ability to draw from any of those areas should give you a level of confidence that propels you into a stellar performance. That said, nothing takes the place of good old-fashioned preparation. In real estate, when Alexandra McCauley has a listing appointment, she spends time educating herself beforehand on the client, the neighborhood, and the property. Engineers like Anthony are known for their preparation. In his world, he plays out the different paths of any discussion, meeting, or interview he may encounter. This enables him to develop a strategy to counter those possibilities, thus giving him the confidence he needs to take the stage. I'll give the last bit of wisdom shine to the late Sanford "Sandy" Meisner. No need to give you his full bio because the man has an acting technique named after him that's been used by the likes of Amy Schumer, Tom Cruise, and several others. Sandy is quoted as saying, "Acting is behaving truthfully under imaginary circumstances." Doing the work gets you the confidence. Confidence gets you in the right frame of mind to take the stage. Once on the stage, allow your personhood to meld with the current circumstances, causing your audience to be delighted. From those who do it well, that's how you deliver a stellar performance.

FACT

Every day you take the stage. Long gone are the days when the only stage you could find was in the cafeteria of an elementary school. The theater is no longer the only place to catch a good performance. Just retrace the history. Radio dramas became television shows, which became movie productions, which have become YouTube channels. For some of today's social media celebrities, their stage could be their living room, the passenger seat of a car, a table at a restaurant, and my all-time favorite, the gym. Stages also include everything from an e-mail to a webinar to a group presentation. It can be a school hallway, a conference room, a networking event, or an interview. In the course of a day, you'll find yourself on multiple stages with different audiences. In the morning, your stage is your home. Minutes later your stage becomes a classroom or office. Later that day, your stage is a lunch table. At some point, your stage will be a dialogue over the telephone. Occasionally, your stage will be a bit more demanding if you find yourself in front of someone that will be judging you: your boss, a client, an interviewer, or your peers. Here's what I want you to take away from this. Fact: the moment you leave your home it's lights, camera, action, showtime. You're onstage, and your audience is watching. Don't ever allow yourself to think otherwise. Since all that is fact, I implore you to live by this rule. This is your show. You're the writer, producer, and director; and the leading role is yours. That said, it's your responsibility as a performer to give them a show they'll always remember.

Now that we've firmly established that you're always onstage, we need to address the next fact: motivation. For some it's money; for others, survival. Then there is a smaller group of people that are motivated by what they see as providing a service. They take the stage so we can be entertained. And we pay a handsome fee for that service. Occasionally, you come across those that are motivated to take on a different personality just as a means of escape. Their real life fails to give them the satisfaction they crave, so they create a new one. Yet for most of us, we're motivated with simple hopes of being considered, recognized, appreciated, and valued. Stage presence here is used to bring a level of professional currency in the form of promotions, raises, or credibility. Fact: motivation moves us to act. In all these scenarios, the key is having a driving force to become (and not fake) another persona. Once that reason is revealed, all that's left is to practice until you can give an Oscar-winning performance.

You were born with acting in your DNA. As children, we're all imitators of those around us. We take on the personality of parents. We adopt habits of our friends and make them our own. We mimic traits of those we idolize on television and fuse them into our personal world. Fact: you've been acting every day from a young age, and it spills over into your work life. The person you are at work is not fully the person you are at home—not completely. You "act" one way in front of your colleagues and a completely different way around family and friends. If you acted all corporate and serious in casual settings, they'd kick you to the curb with the quicks. On the flip side, if you acted as nonchalant with your coworkers, clients, or management as you do with your friends, you wouldn't be taken as seriously and would risk losing your audience.

Remember having fantasies of being a fairytale princess or a superhero? Our imaginations were powerful forces that provoked us to put on that ~~pillowcase~~ cape and pretend to fly around the house. Nothing in the world could tell us that our feet were still on the ground. In our minds, we had taken flight. Some of us had an uncanny ability to transform the interior of our bedroom into a majestic sitting room fit for royalty. Throw in a stately accent and voilà, you were Mary Queen of Scotts. This brings me to my next fact.

Belief is critical. We played the role of princess or superhero so well because deep down inside, we believed we were or would one day be Cinderella or Superman. Without belief, you *are* merely faking until you make it. When you have an undeniable conviction that makes your audience believe every word that comes out of your mouth—that you are not a poor excuse for a cliché or a false representation of the truth—that's when you're becoming one with the role. That's the sweet spot. Think about it. When you see a stellar performance from your favorite actor/actress, you don't say they're faking it. Why? Because they make you believe they and the character are one person. Some people have watched a film and have permanently replaced the name of the performer with the character they portrayed. I'm sure you've watched a movie or TV show where the person did such a good job bringing a character to life that you now refer to them by that character's name. I have. Faye Dunaway is forever Mommy Dearest. I don't even know the real name of the person that plays Agent Smith (*The Matrix*). What's the guy's name that plays T'Challa (*Black Panther*)? Yeah, him. Then, of course, there's Emma Watson who has played other roles, but c'mon, you only know her as Hermione Granger (*Harry Potter*). I read where Jack Nicholson warned Heath Ledger about letting the role of the Joker consume him. Some actors/actresses are so proficient at becoming someone else that we've created emotional feelings toward them simply based on how well they played a certain role. My mom stopped watching

The Brady Bunch because the actor that played Mike Brady, the dad, also played Dr. William Reynolds, a slave owner, in the miniseries *Roots*. How is this level of performance achieved? How do they get us to believe? It goes back to that one word: practice.

Yes, we're talking about practice. You have to do the work before you deliver the performance. To validate this fact, I'd like to draw your attention to the one thing every successful actor/actress does prior to taking the stage or filming. They submerge themselves in an enormous amount of study time. Countless hours, weeks, even months, and sometimes years are spent learning about the character. Research is required to get a feel for the environment the character is a part of. A good actor/actress will exhaust every possible resource to walk in someone else's shoes—a task that is commonly known to be impossible. All this is done well before the director yells, "ACTION!" Charlize Theron committed five months to researching the life of Aileen Wuornos in order to "become" the serial killer in the movie *Monster*. Her preparation earned her an Oscar award for the Best Actress in a Leading Role in 2003. In 2005, Jamie Foxx took home an Oscar, a Golden Globe, and a BAFTA (British Academy of Film and Television Arts) award for his leading role in *Ray*. How did he "become" one with Ray Charles? Simple. He had his eyes glued shut for fourteen hours a day to experience a microcosm of the life of a blind person. I can hear Allen Iverson yelling…"Practice!"

"But, Rodney, those are movie stars. That's their profession. They've been doing that kind of work for years. They have access to people that can help them with their craft." You're absolutely right. So let's look at someone a bit more inconspicuous. Ever heard of Joe Pistone? Take a moment to look him up, and you'll see striking similarities to the preparation taken by these posh celebrities. Beginning in 1976, Joe Pistone played the role of Donnie Brasco for six years. His character's objective was to infiltrate one of the five main Mafia families in NYC. His audience was mobsters and criminals. In order to get them to believe his character was real, he studied the characteristics of a typical mobster. He learned that he had to be exceptionally talented at telling lies. He needed to understand the rules of the Mafia world. He needed to convince them that he belonged. To do this, he presented himself as a small-time jewelry thief. He had to commit to learning that game as well. He spent two weeks learning the jewelry industry. The FBI.gov website says that "Pistone had fooled them all with a masterful acting job…" Uh, yeah! He couldn't afford not to. A bad review meant severe consequences. It's far more serious than tomatoes or social media bashing—pun intended (mobsters do a different kind of bashing). This performance was literally life or death. In the end, Joe didn't take home a shiny trophy. There was no awards ceremony to celebrate his work. There was, however, a payoff. It started with over one hundred federal convictions. Joe's acting job was the catalyst for decades of work that aided the FBI in taking down major criminal organizations.

To summarize, remember the following points:

1. Life is a stage. You're always on. If your audience is looking for a show, why not give them a good one?
2. In acting spaces, there's a common punch line, "What's my motivation?" You have to have a reason. Find that reason, and let it be the driving force that causes you to "become" a different version of yourself without losing who you are.
3. You've been here before. Principles are transferrable. The same thought process you employed as a child to become a princess or a superhero is the same process you use to get noticed in the professional world.
4. If you don't believe you belong, neither will your audience. This is where you move from faking it to becoming one with the role of manager, executive, business mogul, or whatever you're aspiring to become.
5. Practice doesn't make perfect. Deliberate practice is what you should strive for. You have to put in the work before you go onstage. Do the research, study the part, have some dress rehearsals. When the time is right, you'll be ready. You'll give a stellar performance. Your audience will applaud, leaving nothing else for you to do but take a bow.

CHAPTER 5

The B-Side

"His words carry weight that would break a less
interesting man's jaw. He is, indeed, the most
interesting man in the world."
—William "Will" Lyman, voice of
the Dos Equis commercials

An essential part of Corporate Swagger is having an aura about you that is so captivating that it lures people in. It's like when you're riding down the street and the smell of flame-grilled beef makes you bust a U-turn. Next thing you know, you're ordering a #7 combo meal. This kind of fascination works like crankbait on the end of a fishing line. Having this kind of attraction puts you in position to catch the big one. You'll know you've achieved it when people are curious to know more about you and find themselves in awe of anything you share with them. Sound difficult? It's not. It requires some work, but you can do this. That's what this chapter is all about. You'll learn how to own the room without paying for it. I love the proverb in the bible that says, "Don't work yourself into the spotlight. Don't push your way into the place of prominence. It's better to be promoted to a place of honor." That's what I mean by not paying for it. This component of Corporate Swagger is not about forcing yourself into the spotlight. It's about knowing how to make the spotlight find you and how to conduct yourself once it does. The secret to doing that is found on your B-side.

What is a B-side? To answer that we first need to make sure you know where it's found. Technological advancements in music have made this phrase as outdated as saying, "I need to buy some film for my camera." Go back with me before streaming music, before MP3 players, before CDs. The year is 1963 and cassette tapes (tapes, for short) have just emerged on to the music scene. This palm-sized rectangular object concealed a miniature reel-to-reel mechanism. One reel would contain a spool of thin brown tape. As the reels turned, the spool of tape would transfer from one reel to the other. While passing from reel to reel, the tape would softly pass over a square piece of felt. Some kind of way, this would cause the music that was imprinted on the tape to be played and heard. That was way too much of an explanation. Just YouTube it. The cassette tape had two sides: an A side, usually considered the front or primary side, and a B side—the back or secondary side. Once one side was finished playing, you'd have to eject the cassette, flip it over, then reinsert it and press *play*.

The artist reserved the A side for the songs they intended to be more mainstream. These were the tracks you'd hear on the radio and the same ones that would serve as the primary identity of the album. The most notable songs including the title track would often be found on the A side. Since nothing an artist creates is junk, that's not to imply that the opposite side was a place for the lyrical leftovers or musical scraps. The songs on the flip side aren't bad or inferior in quality by any means. For the most part, the songs on the B side added substance to the entire work. Some producers would place instrumentals, remixes, or behind-the-scenes footage on the B side. Occasionally, you'd get a bonus track. Every artist or production studio always had a strategy or a purpose for the B side. "Rodney, what does this have to do with me? I'm not a musician. We don't use cassette tapes anymore. I'm trying to get a promotion." It has everything to do with you. There's a principle that must be respected when attempting to craft your corporate game. There's only so much you can do in the shallow end of the pool. Eventually, people will want to go deeper. When that time comes, you better have some-thing else for them to latch on to or else you'll find yourself taking an L. Consider the next four chapters as the second-half game plan after coming out of the locker room. The first half was about establishing the basics. Now it's time to run up the score. This is how you take your Corporate Swagger to the next level.

Your A side is equivalent to what people expect to see when you show up. Your A side is written on your résumé. Your A side is usu-ally what gets noticed first. It can include (but isn't limited to) your business attire, eloquent speaking, educational background, work experience…yada-yada, blah-zay-blah. It's the surface-level stuff. It's all valuable and necessary, so don't change any of it! Your A side is the calling card that opens the door for the opportunity you're hoping to take advantage of. However, when that side is finished playing—that is, when your surface-level qualities have done their job and the music stops—then what? You're going to have to take them deeper. When they flip the tape over, they better like what they hear.

Your B side is the side that doesn't show up on your résumé. It may be on your résumé tucked underneath the "hobbies and inter-ests" section, but without your ability to narrate the story and fill in the gaps, they're just nice asides on a piece of paper. Your B side can't be seen through your nice business attire. This part of your corporate game transcends your objective, GPA, work experience, and other predictable sections of your résumé. It's much deeper than nice eye color, exquisite taste in shoes, or a dope sock game. You want your B side to be the recording that everyone is playing over and over in their head all day. You want them reciting every interesting fact about you long after you're gone. Your intent is to own a portion of real estate in their minds. Your B side sits hidden in plain sight until that opportune moment. You'll know the spotlight has found you when you hear, "I would have never known that about you. How interest-ing. Tell me more." Your B side is the aura that compels people to engage with you. This is the part of your game that obligates your audience to take notice and, better yet, remember you.

For instance, everyone wants to talk to Calvin who leaves the office Friday evening only to find himself suspended from the side of a mountain later that weekend because Calvin enjoys freestyle rock climbing. Monday, Calvin is back in the office in business attire like everyone else. The difference between the average one-hit wonder and Calvin is that…Calvin has a B side. Or consider Yvette. Jaws will drop when they find out that she has been a competitive gamer for the past several years and is sponsored by a major corporation. The difference is her flip side has tracks that no one saw coming. It takes a certain level of vulnerability to disclose parts of your nonbusiness persona in professional settings. But this is the special VIP/backstage experience your audience is craving. Be mindful to deliver it with a sense of humility because no one likes a show-off. These tracks are what separate the person that no one can remember from the person that becomes the topic of conversation with influencers, decision-makers, and higher-ups. Congratulations, you've just purchased the room without buying it.

EXPERIENCE

I used to be a recruiter for a top firm in the industry. It was a Wednesday evening sometime after 5:00 PM, and I had no reason to rush home. Why sit in an empty apartment, right? Instead, I'll sit in the place I've spent the last 8+ hours. That makes sense. This particular evening, I overheard a couple of my coworkers having a conversation about what one of them did the previous weekend. I couldn't tell you the details of the conversations, but one thing resonated with me. One of the ladies said, "😲 Wow, you did what?"

At that moment I asked myself, "When was the last time someone had that kind of response after I told them about my weekend?" It didn't take me long to search my mental database because it had never happened. Yeah, couldn't find anything. More than one third of my life lived and not one experience to point to that ever made the room stop and take notice—nothing.

That night I decided to put into motion what I would later call my wow moment. Being fresh off a divorce and living in a $590-studio apartment, I decided it was time to spend some money. I logged on to one of the travel sites and found the last-minute deals link. It was like finding the travel site's B side tracks. Anyway, I came across a weekend trip: round trip air and hotel to Belize for $298. You'll laugh at this, but I didn't even know where Belize was. I had to look it up on the internet. I researched the hotel, and it was a small one-bedroom beach-side bungalow. I may have read a review or two, maybe not. All I knew was I'd get a chance to have my passport stamped, go to a place I didn't know existed, and celebrate my new relationship status. That Wednesday night I booked the trip. Friday after work I headed to the airport. By 7:00 PM CST, I was on an island in another country, chillaxing in a bungalow on the beach. Did I mention I took this excursion BY MYSELF? Yeah, there I was walking the streets of Ambergris Caye, taking in the sights, doing a speedboat tour, eating with the locals, gettin' it in for two days. As an unexpected bonus to the itinerary, I even found myself in a taxi with a driver that needed to make a street pharmaceutical delivery to a friend of his in a quaint dark alley. Translation: cab driver decided to make a drug run while I was in the car. Oh yeah, it went down like that.

Monday morning, I showed up to work and just waited. Again, it's about letting the spotlight find you. I knew my time would come because it's the questions everyone asks on Monday morning. C'mon, you know it. Say it with me, "How was your weekend?" Had I been waiting for this moment? You bet I had. All I had to do was say that I booked a last-minute trip to Belize and BAM! Jaws hit the floor and the room stopped. Then I heard those magic words: "Wow! You did what?" Check, please. We're done here. I don't know what they say in a recording studio after laying down the perfect track, but that's exactly how I felt.

With that experience, I was able to add to my B side tracks. Prior to that I had nothing to give my audience should the spotlight find itself on me. Since then, I've played that cut (shared that story) in a few settings. It gets the same response every time. In addition, it has helped check additional boxes that translate in the workplace:

- ✓ Willing to take calculated risks
- ✓ Can make tough decisions
- ✓ Able to function outside of comfort zone

☑ Creative problem solver
☑ Adventurous and likes to have fun

These were all points that gave me a competitive advantage in business settings, interviews, and networking events. I couldn't rest on that one alone. I needed to find a way to add more tracks. As in any game, if you don't evolve, you'll soon be passed by your competition. That's when I noticed I had overlooked a few things that carried some weight: classically trained opera singer who can sing in multiple languages—I was a music major in college, and I can sing classical music in Latin, Italian, German, and other languages; OCR (Obstacle Course Racer)—my wife and I have been avid Spartan race runners since 2015, totaling seventeen races to date (and counting); on the board of directors for a national nonprofit—I sit on the board for the Houston region of Big Brothers Big Sisters of America; currently learning to speak Korean—my wife is half Korean, and it's a goal of mine to be able to speak to her family in their language. This isn't to promote my B side. This is to help you identify some possible tracks you have just lying around collecting dust. Put those things to use and add them to your repertoire. Like I said, with a little bit of work, you can begin to sculpt multiple facets of yourself that appeal to a wide array of audiences. It's simple. Don't just work out. Work out with a greater purpose. Don't just volunteer. Seek a position of leadership. Don't just learn a new language. Have a predetermined function for the language. Don't just travel. Go do something that makes people say, "Wow!" The point is don't do things purely out of requirement. That's the purpose of your A side. Instead, take the time to be acutely involved in something interesting. See it as an investment in your professional street cred. Find something that intrigues you, then have the curiosity to go deeper.

At this point in the game, everyone has credentials: degree, experience, and licenses. What used to separate people in the workplace now causes congestion. Finding that unique quality is like looking at a sea of gray and hoping to identify the one person in red. In my working years of identifying talent, the one thing that separates one from another is not surface-level evaluations. When all things are equal and the tale of the tape is a mirror image on both sides, decision-makers are forced to look for that concealed quality that sets one person apart from the other. When the odds rest on a 50/50 chance and your technical skill set has been exhausted, then what? When your résumé, work experience, and certifications have bored them to death, how do you make them a fan of your work? It all comes back to the bait you use. Simply eject the tape, flip it over, and let them hear what's on your B side.

WISDOM

We've all been asked, "Tell me something about you I don't know." When you read between the lines, what they're really saying is tell me something interesting about you. Explain the importance of having depth to your character that compels people to engage with you.

I learned things about friends and close acquaintances that I would have never imagined—all because I asked them to take me into the booth where they recorded some of their best B side tracks. It was this topic that caused me to thank each person in the most heartfelt way for their contribution to this project simply because of how vulnerable they allowed themselves to be. At times during many conversations, I forgot I was interviewing them and was, all of a sudden, prisoner to my very own tactic. They had done to me exactly what you'll need to do to your audience if you want to achieve this level of Corporate Swagger.

Get this right, and your audience will sway to the cadence of everything you have to say. Get it wrong, and it's like Courtney told me, "Looks and charisma will only get you so far. It's easy to come into the office with high heels and lipstick…but if you're not a person of substance, all the flare gets harder and harder to maintain." One of my friends in talent acquisition was pretty adamant when she cautioned those that think yesterday's game will get them tomorrow's trophy. Her words were, "Some people come out of school with this 'I was homecoming queen, top 10 percent in my class' mentality, and now you show up in a room where others are just as beautiful and just as smart. You will get your butt handed to you. You may have thought you were the queen bee. Now you're in there with all the queen bees." If that isn't a public service announcement that makes you focus on creating a deeper level to your game, I don't know what is. Both of them also agree that faking it till you make it is a flawed game plan. It may have worked before; but people are looking for a more genuine connection, and everybody has a BS meter. Here's how to make sure it doesn't start beeping when you come into the room.

It's fitting to set the stage with a story that Charles shared with me. He had just received a promotion to assistant general manager. Everyone on his team was at least fifteen years his senior with years more experience. In normal fashion, he would address his team with the typical business items that needed to be completed in order to make business better. He noticed that his team wasn't responsive to his requests and that the work wasn't getting done. Concerned about the output and the lack of responsibility, he sought wisdom. Side note: let that be a nugget in itself. Don't let pride get in the way of reaching out for help. Don't be so high on your status or title that you can't humble yourself to seek someone else's guidance. Now back to our regularly scheduled program. Charles approached a trusted colleague in the human resources department. He explained the situation he was dealing with in hopes of walking away with a solution that would help to whip his team into shape. To his surprise, he was given advice on fixing himself...and not his team. He was told that despite his intellect; his system savvy; his aptitude on files, forecasts, and manpower planning, there was one critical area of deficiency. "They don't know you," she said. That wisdom falls directly in line with Theodore Roosevelt's famous quote, "Nobody cares how much you know until they know how much you care."

Charles took the advice and made the adjustments to become more personable. Eventually, things started clicking with everyone on his team, and work was getting done as he initially hoped. That experience taught him that having a strong B side for his audience to listen to meant caring about people. It's a summation of the characteristics beneath you that go beyond "How much did we get done today?" His notes from that lesson are below:

1. Be a person of character.
2. Know what drives you.
3. Don't be a one-trick pony.

Other comments on this subject all carried the same idea that also links to the lesson Charles learned. It's all about making a human connection with people. Steven Coleman relies on having a diverse portfolio of personhood to make sure he increases his chances of making the connection. He accomplishes this by being well-rounded in a number of areas: the arts, sports, literature, current affairs, and most of all, intricate aspects of his own journey. He says that when you operate from a broad base of personhood, you'll be well versed to handle any type of discussion.

This theory rings true when we look at Sarah Bolka's B side. Her tracks include being a former Marine Corps officer and her love of singing along with how she's run two Ironman races and that she scuba dives. It is a wide array of *personhood* that allows her to make human connections on multiple levels. She can draw from any one of those tracks or principles contained within them to become one with her audience. She believes so deeply in this ability that she named her daughter Arete, which (in Greek) means "well-rounded excellence." By definition, a person of *arete* is of the highest effectiveness; they use all their faculties. I know Greece is approximately seven hundred miles from Rome, but the saying is still true: "When in Rome, do as the Romans do." I also found it interesting that Sarah, like Tyra, offered up a couple things to keep at the forefront: (1) She said to be interested in other people's B side. She sees that people miss opportunities to make that human connection because they may feel pressure to talk about themselves; (2) Don't pretend to adopt someone else's B side. Be confident in your own because in the corporate environment, this is what will set you apart.

Darryl Blackburn spoke to the depth of character when we talked about this. He said, "The deeper someone's character, the larger their network will be." His rule is to never do passions alone. When I asked him what he meant by that, he explained that if you have so many interests/passions and you can connect with different people on all those, you'll always have a network that's working in your favor. I found what he shared with me next to be a very calculated. He said, "For every one of my passions, I have a separate network. Each one displays the depth of my character and breadth of network." 😬 Okay. I took that to mean the best way to grow your network is to have multiple interests. With each interest comes a different set of people to network with. Having more B side tracks can, in turn, create a tidal wave of associates and friends that can be called on when in need of professional assistance. Brilliant!

Let's say the endgame to having a good B side is about creating a sense of team. It works there as well. Veronica's approach to playing her B side is all about transparency. She believes that people want to know if the relationship is going to be more than just a transaction. The way she goes about making the human connection is by serving up slices of her interests with those she wants to influence. She'll intentionally share articles with colleagues and managers that go beyond job-related content to help drive the conversation and connection. It's common practice for her to send an e-mail of a *NYT* article, a *Washington Post* write-up, or a CNBC link that shines a light on something she finds interesting. She's careful to play the role of Switzerland as not to ruffle any feathers. Don't go sending political commentary to your boss. That's not what she's saying. Her goal is not to incite e-mail beefs but to give her audience a peephole into her deeper character. However, she's not afraid to get vulnerable and share aspects of her personal life as well. In the right settings, she gives way to the fact that she's studying French or shares an excerpt from a book she's reading or delights her audience with a tale from a recent travel adventure. Her approach is simple: "The more you share with others, the more they feel they can reach out and connect." This same approach is shared by someone else I talked to in talent acquisition. She told me that if you just do the grind, life is boring; it's important to be able to talk about subjects unrelated to work because, in her field, that's how you win business.

I want to make sure that we don't lose sight of the purpose behind developing this side of you. First and foremost, as everyone has stated and as I'll reiterate, this is not about faking it or being someone you're not. This is about becoming multifaceted so that you can perform at an optimal level at the drop of a dime. That said, it's important to develop this quality with the end in mind and also stay cognizant of some of the pitfalls of a negative B side.

Perspective is a beautiful teacher. It allows for fresh insight and takes you into the hidden thought patterns of someone else's mind. I mention that because when I talked to Tyra Metoyer, she was one of the first who approached this topic from a different vantage point. She agreed with everyone else about the importance of having a B side. But out of nowhere, she hit me with this idea of having a negative B side. I remember being on the phone with her when she said it, and I had a college relapse. It was like being in a lecture class when the professor hits on something that you know is going to show up on the final, so your note-taking skills go into a higher gear. She explained that sometimes what lurks beneath someone's surface layer is a super direct person that is prone to hurt people's feelings. You may be someone that just wants to get the job done so you're not as sensitive to others. She went on to say, "Sometimes in the throes of trying to get stuff done, I'm not thinking about that [being nice or catering to someone's feelings], and that's not always the best way to be." Having keen emotional intelligence keeps her mindful of making sure people see less of her negative B side and more of her positive.

Let's say you're in business for yourself and you need to recruit the efforts of others. Or perhaps you're in a situation where you need to influence people. Having a compelling B side will help. Alexandra McCauley banks on it. Her level of understanding in this area didn't surprise me when considering her degree in communication and media studies from UC Santa Barbara. She's built a successful referral-based real estate career in a competitive market because she has an appreciation for all forms of communication. That includes knowing when to flip the tape over and let the audience hear something that takes them deeper. Like Tyra, her EQ meter is also sensitive to coming off the wrong way. In her business, she says, you can get personal with people very quickly. Knowing that, she's methodical with how she goes about it. Her tactic is to share an equal amount of information that her client is willing to share. This allows her to sidestep any awkward-moment landmines during the interaction. Unfortunately, she can't say that for some of her clients. In her words, "If you're not careful, you can expose your own ignorance and risk losing Corporate Swagger points." She went on to share with me that "It always cracks me up when people make racial comments to me. They think because I'm a white girl from California that I'm good with it. They end up making a complete fool of themselves because what they don't know is that I'm Jewish and I'm married to a black man." Prime example of how being so self-indulged and emotionally unintelligent can expose your negative B side and bite you in the butt if you're not careful.

It was fascinating to hear Thoma's take on how to make this connection. He uses authenticity to amplify his B side. He had me at hello when he opened up by saying, "There is falsity in men." It doesn't take much deliberation to agree that we all want to look good in the eyes of others. That's why you're reading this book, and that's all right. It does bring about a different perspective to be questioned. When you lay yourself on the operating table and allow others to see what's really going on inside, will they still want to connect? In this social media age, it's the equivalent of using filters when you know your face has a few imperfections. Or when you were little you would eagerly tell your parents about the A you made on the history test but conveniently overlook the times you failed the other tests. You get my point. We're all Superman in our own eyes.

If that's the case, then Thoma is Bizarro. His B side is laced with tracks that uncover his losses (more than his wins) and the lessons learned from dealing with them. He has a knack for captivating his audience with "school of hard knocks" parables that point to things he learned from his father, the passing of a close friend, or even something that happened at home with his family. This is his way of letting you know his character and his drive. Neither of which can be determined with 100 percent accuracy by surface observation alone. He put a nice bow on this part of our conversation when he said, "To me it's how you look at me holistically versus how you see me on the surface." When it's all said and done, we all want more. More of everything. Having authentic human interaction is not exempt.

Here's a bonus track straight from the kitchen of Chef B. If you're familiar with the phrase "Loose lips sink ships," then you're also familiar with how Byrena uses this concept of the B side. She revealed one of her interviewing strategies is to get so comfortable with people (by sharing her B side) and make them equally as comfortable that they just start talking about themselves in a casual way. Her aim is to give them the opportunity to expose any potential cracks in their ship that could ultimately lead to them sinking—and not getting the job. What do I mean? She's trained herself to pinpoint all the following when people share their B side during an interview:

- Reliability
- Integrity
- Sense of honesty
- Problem solving
- Quick-tempered
- Coachable

It's like Anthony told me, "What you're getting at is something core about the individual." Byrena is looking for pieces of the candidate's puzzle that she can put together to give her an accurate depiction of whether they deserve the job or not. She'll ask questions that get them out of interview mode and on to the operating table. She says that she wants to see their passion come through their conversation. When they do that, they can't stop talking. Next thing you know, they've taken off the filters and she has a chance to evaluate the real person.

The B side can make or break you. With that in mind, it makes sense to grab ahold of this last piece of wisdom she left me with. "I used to gauge my success on how hard I was working, but I realized that was surface. I realized there are other aspects (family, friends, football, school) that I can use to make myself more valuable. It's never too late to invest in yourself and add layers. Recognize that the best part of you is what makes you different from everyone else." The best part of you is your B side.

FACT

Most of us have been there. It could have been an interview. It may have been a business presentation. Maybe it was on a first or second date. It happens after your A side is finished playing. You've given them everything you think they need to know about you in order to come to a decision. You put it all out there on your résumé, in your PowerPoint, or on your social media profile. What more could they ask? Then they hit you with "So tell me something about you that I don't already know." They're all asking this question because they're interested in knowing more about the person behind the facade. They want you to take them deeper. They want a sense for the side of you that only special people get to see. That side reserved for those in your inner circle. Ultimately, they're requesting what we all want when we meet someone with a good A side. Give us exclusive access that makes us feel special. If you read between the lines, the real request is for you to share something about yourself that may cause them to lean in a bit further. None of what they're looking for is traditional. None of it is typical. All of that is found on your B side. If you can't fulfil that request, game over.

- If it's an interview: "Thanks for coming. We're going to go in a different direction."
- If it's a business proposition: "Your presentation was excellent. We'll keep you in mind."
- If it's a social interaction: "I don't know if I'll be available. I think I may be sick next weekend."

If there was a language that epitomized swagger, it would be French. If there was a phrase that summed up Corporate Swagger, it would be *je ne sais quoi* (French for "I don't know what"). It's that pleasant and indescribable trait that causes people to gravitate toward you. Sorry, but my native tongue was derived from the South Side of

Chicago, so I refer to it as Cool-AID. For the sake of keeping things simple, I'm going to focus on three bite-size pieces and a nifty way to remember them.

Attraction—we're taking the limits off and going well beyond appearance. Trust me, if it were all about looks, I'd have very little to offer. I mentioned it earlier, but you must possess a mysterious aura that lifts people off their feet and has them floating in your direction. There has to be an element to your game that's attractive. What will grab your audience and pull them closer?

Impression—there's no sense in being attractive if once you have them in your web, they have no reason to stay engaged with you. Leaving an impression is all about creating a lasting memory and making them feel good about the interaction. This is the stuff that creates fans for life.

Delivery—so you've attracted them; you have material you feel will keep them interested. Now it's time to deliver it. Here we're talking about the art of storytelling. As humans we're drawn to a good story. Stories appeal to the imagination; they paint pictures; they move audiences. A quality delivery leads to a standing ovation. In the business world that means you get called back for another interview. Neither of these things leave the desired impact when left to mere words on paper. However, the impact is tenfold when skillfully deployed in a social or professional setting. Get your shovel. Let's do some digging into each one of these and unearth the cold hard facts.

Studies as well as your own observations have proven that attraction is not always about the superficial aspects. Looks will become secondary when measured against similarities. I know, I know…opposites attract. Well, we're not talking about magnets right now. Fact: we're drawn to those like us. Scientifically, there have been countless studies in this area. I was reading about one of them in the *Journal of Personality and Social Psychology*. Researchers asked more than 150 participants to read questionnaires that had been allegedly completed by other unknown participants referred to as "bogus strangers." After reading the responses from the stranger, the participants were asked to rate their attraction based on those responses. The questionnaire focused on normal attitudinal tendencies (e.g., premarital sex, television programs, etc.). What they found was that 70 percent of the participants found the bogus stranger to be attractive purely based on similarities. The key here is that we don't even know if real people filled these questionnaires out. What we do know is that the participants did not have looks to base their attraction on. Yet an overwhelming majority of people experienced a level of attraction.

From a business perspective, how much weight does a professional matchmaker put into facial features, biceps, or cup size (male or female cup size)? Sure, they'll consider looks, but it isn't the driving factor. For the most part, their business model is based on an algorithm that analyzes written/typed responses on an application that is matched to someone else's responses. Once they have a match on paper, they bring both parties in for separate interviews where the potential matches get to play their B side. It's during these interviews that the decision is made. Again, the other person isn't even in the room. Next thing you know, two strangers are going on a date.

Common sense says when you ask someone what kind of qualities they'd want in a mate, you'd be hard pressed to find someone that describes their opposite. Imagine for a second. You're a foodie who enjoys hiking and spending time with family. Would you say your ideal mate would be a couch potato who prefers to spend holidays alone and has the palate of child who orders chicken tenders and fries at an upscale restaurant? Not at all. Still need proof that attraction isn't all about looks. I'm not going to name any names, but when I make this point, you'll undoubtedly have someone in mind. Have you ever seen two people together seemingly in love or married and ask yourself, "🫤 🫥 🫨 How'd that happen?" I'll wait… I rest my case, Your Honor. If you'll approach attractiveness from a standpoint of similarities. Statistically, you can "look" amazing. It's been proven. People want to be around those they feel they have a connection to. Vulnerability is your best asset. Your job is to become a sleuth and uncover those similarities. This allows others to see beneath the surface. Similarity forms the connection. Similarity activates the "Gilroy." Similarity is your aura.

Don't get too lazy with this. There's still some work that needs to be done once you've identified similarities. You can't just sit there playing the "me too" game forever. "You like to travel? Me too." "You have a dog? Me too." The interaction will require a deeper level of engagement if you're going to keep them interested.

I'm not going to insult you by spouting a bunch of clichés about making an impression. You already know how long you have to do that. Plus, you don't need another lecture on the consequences of making a bad one. That's not what we want to address here. You want to know the how-to behind said clichés. Rather than give you the whole ten-steps-to-recovery list of things to do, I'm only going to focus on one. That's right. The goal here is not to have you checking endless boxes worried if you hit them all. No, I want you to be able to go into your next business setting and put this to work tomorrow! At first thought, the way to go about it is completely opposite of what you'd expect. You would think that in order to have people remember you, you would need to tell them everything about you: how you conquered the world, how smart you are, the school you went to, work experience, shoe size, favorite teddy bear's name, etc. Please don't. You'll get talked about as soon as you're not around. If you want to leave the most indelible impression, all you need to do is be curious about others. Make the interaction more about them than it is about you. Fact: to quote Maya Angelou, "I've learned that people will forget what you said, people will forget what you did, but people will never forget how you made them feel." How do you make someone feel good? Easy. Put *them* in the spotlight. I remember reading *The Charisma Myth* by Olivia Fox Cabane. She opens with an account of William Gladstone and Benjamin Disraeli. They were opponents for UK Prime Minister in 1886. Before the election, both men just so happened to entertain the same lady for dinner—separately, of course. When asked, the young lady mentioned that after spending time with Mr. Gladstone, it was evident that he was the cleverest person in England. After spending time with Mr. Disraeli, she thought she was the cleverest person in England. Not because he was unintelligent. It was because he was smart enough to put her in the spotlight. Spoiler alert: Mr. Disraeli won the election. Curiosity is how you make an unforgettable impression. Be interested in someone other than yourself. Learn about your audience. Serve them. Make them feel special. You'll have plenty of time to be in the spotlight, but if you want to stay there, I suggest you share it.

The US National Library of Medicine and National Institutes of Health cites three studies done by Todd Kashdan of the Department of Psychology at George Mason University. One in particular proved that curiosity has a positive outcome in social settings where complete strangers are interacting with one another. The exercise included one "confederate" (this is a trained person working in concert with the person/people doing the research without the participants knowing) and ninety-eight college students. The confederate and each student would be paired and given a set of questions to ask each other in a 1:1 conversation. The confederate's instructions from the researcher was to provide the same answers to each participant despite their responses. Afterward both people would rate how attracted and how close they felt to the person they were conversing with. Results showed that the confederates were more attracted to participants that were curious than those that weren't. Likewise, participants that were curious felt they made a memorable impression on the confederate more than those that weren't curious.

In a second study by Kashdan consisting of ninety complete strangers, participants were asked to have small talk with one another. Again, more curious people felt closer to their conversation partner; less curious people had a lesser experience with the closeness they felt. "When you show curiosity and you ask questions and find out something interesting about another person, people disclose more, share more, and they return the favor, asking questions of you," says Kashdan. "It sets up a spiral of give and take, which fosters intimacy," he said. The facts don't lie. When you make the interaction more about your audience than you, you navigate a path of closeness and connectivity even with complete strangers. This level of communication is what has your audience remembering you long after you've left their presence. You become the song in their head they can't stop humming.

Both attraction and impression are amplified by your delivery. Can you tell a good story? Are you able to paint a picture with your words that takes your audience to a place they've never been? Will your listener(s) buy what you're selling? Plainly said, can you move the crowd? With the proper delivery, you can leave an impression that gives them memory burn. Imagine a spider spinning a web. The spider excretes oils that allow it to effortlessly glide across the web like an ice skater floats on the ice. Unfortunately, the same can't be said for anything caught in the web. To them, it acts as a snare. In this analogy, you're the spider, your story is the oil, and your delivery is the web.

Stories are a means to connect with people. The strength of the connection depends on the emotional attachment the storyteller has to what it is they're sharing. What I mean by that is when you tell a story that happened to you, the emotional attachment level is at its highest. Contrasted by when you tell a story that happened to someone you don't know or have never met, it's hard to conjure the same level of emotion in your delivery. Without the emotion, the connection is weakened. Another way to maintain the strength in the connection is by being transparent. When you take your audience beneath the surface into an area of your life that is reserved for a select few, you put yourself in position to create a common bond. Because you're delivering it from a firsthand perspective and you're being vulnerable, you can reach back into the raw emotion of the moment and use that as the oil on the web that captivates your listeners. When done correctly, your objective is achieved. Like an insect caught in a web, now you got 'em. You've successfully executed the delivery, thus completing the trifecta: attraction through similarities, an impression they can't forget, delivering a story that moves the crowd.

If you're looking for more scientific facts, I have those too. Fact: there's a hormone in the brain that acts as a neurotransmitter that influences social conduct. It's called oxytocin. This hormone controls how we interact with people and is produced when we are trusted or shown kindness. This tells me that I can change beliefs, alter attitudes, and modify behaviors if I can trigger a flow of oxytocin through a person's system. It's like a highly skilled hacker writing code to take control of someone else's computer. If the brain is our human operating system and we need to hack it, storytelling is the coding language to release the hormone that will cause others to trust you and show you kindness. That means if delivered correctly, you can move people to action. You can essentially influence their decision making to a certain degree. Allow me to introduce you to Paul J. Zak, professor of economic sciences and psychology and management director for the Center for Neuroeconomics Studies. His research has uncovered the process the brain goes through when carrying out empathetic behaviors such as trustworthiness, generosity, and sacrifice—all of which are determinants of likeability. Paul's studies propose that when oxytocin is produced, it motivates cooperation with others. In true scientist fashion, Paul was curious to know if we had the ability to influence oxytocin levels, thus causing a person to be cooperative in a desired area. Results proved that "character-driven stories do consistently cause oxytocin synthesis." He went on to say, "These findings on the neurobiology of storytelling are relevant to business settings. For example, my experiments show that character-driven stories with emotional content result in a better understanding of the key points a speaker wishes to make and enable better recall of these points weeks later." Too much science talk? Let me break it down. You can tell a story that activates a hormone in your audience's brain that causes them to like you. If you include characters and an emotional element, you magnify your attraction and impression. Mic drop! You can put the shovel down now. No more digging necessary. We just struck gold.

There you have it. Now you can say you have them drinking your Cool-AID. You're free from thinking that only the runway models are attractive. You've been given one simple step to making a memorable impression. You struck gold when you learned how to move the crowd with your delivery. The only thing left for you to do is press play. Your B side is ready to be heard.

CHAPTER 6

Pressure Is Privilege

"Smell bad. Heal good."
—Pat Morita as Mr. Miyagi in
The Karate Kid (1984)

What propels your ascension to the level of success you aspire to reach is how you use challenges to your benefit. Insert overused "Don't quit" motivational quote here. I'll do you one better and refer you to a scene from one of my favorite movies, *The Dark Knight Rises*. The writers for this film did an excellent job because I'm sure I'm not alone when I say I draw a considerable amount of inspiration from several lines in this movie.

There was a sequence of scenes where billionaire Bruce Wayne was in jail. That's putting it mildly. Imagine being in the bottom of a well large enough to house a typical prison. The walls were made of earth and stone; the sight of sunlight passes overhead. Each day every prisoner is tempted with a false hope of escaping. How? All they have to do is scale five-hundred feet to the opening of the pit. Accomplish that and the sunlight will greet them with a kiss as they walk triumphantly into freedom's arms. Fail and the only thing keeping them from falling to their demise is a rope attached around their waist. Just a little bit of pressure. By way of cell block story time, Bruce learns there was a child who had been born in that same prison that made the climb to freedom. Why not kick a man when he's down, right?

The billionaire turned prisoner uses that as motivation to make the climb himself, but to no avail. After one of his failed attempts, you can see the pain and disappointment in his body language. Physically unable to walk unassisted, he leans on one of the other prisoners for leverage. Angrily, he barks, "You told me a child did it!" In response to the frustration of his own inability, the prisoner calmly delivers a line that should serve as the reason why you should count yourself as fortunate that you've faced challenges because not everyone has. Surprisingly, they are the unfortunate ones. He says, "No ordinary child…a child born in hell. A child forged by suffering, hardened by pain. Not a man from privilege."

When I thought about how to best illustrate this idea of pressure and how to make it work to your advantage, I thought about this story I read about a potato, an egg, and ground coffee beans. One day there was a young lady that was at her wits end. She kept having struggle after struggle. As soon as she thought she conquered one problem in her life, something else would end up happening. She was in a perpetual crap storm. In search of a pity party, she complained to her dad about how she couldn't seem to get it together. No matter what she did, she just couldn't seem to get her head above water.

In true father fashion, her dad went into fix-it mode. A chef by trade, he decided to teach her a lesson using none other than food. His ingredients of choice: a potato, an egg, and ground coffee beans. He took three identical pots, each filled with the same amount of water, and set them on the stove to boil. Each burner was set to the same degree of heat. In one pot he placed the potato. In the other he put in the egg. In the last pot he poured the ground coffee beans. The father turned on all three burners and patiently waited for them to come to a boil. Of course, the daughter was clueless as to what her father was doing. There's a saying that a watched pot never boils. I can imagine the time it took for the water to come to a boil must have felt like an eternity to his daughter. After letting the boiling process run its course on all three items, the father turned off the burners and took the three ingredients off the stove. He placed the potato on a plate. He put the egg in an egg cup and poured the coffee in a mug. He then asked his daughter, "What do you see?"

She replied, "All I see is the same potato, egg, and coffee."

The father responded, "No. Look again. Look closer." He told her to touch the potato. She noticed the once-hard potato had become soft. He told her to crack the egg open. She noticed the once-fragile egg had become hard. Then he asked her to take a sip of the coffee. The aroma and taste brought a smile to her face.

With childlike curiosity she asked her father, "What does it all mean?" The father explained that we all have challenges in our lives but it's how we use the challenge to help us take the next step in our journey that's important. That only happens when you accept the fact that rain falls on the just and the unjust. We all have problems. We all get caught in storms. We all have our feet held to the fire at some point. Water boils an egg in the same way it boils a potato, which is the same way it boils coffee. What matters is how you use the boiling water (the challenge) to create a different environment.

So now, looking back at this story and whatever it is that has you thinking about tapping out, which ingredient are you? Are you the potato that goes into a situation hard-nosed, thinking you have it all together, only to be weakened by the heat of your circumstances? Are you the raw, naive egg that is fragile and hypersensitive? Anything that goes wrong in your world is a direct attack against you. You crack at the slightest tap on your exterior. We see here that once exposed to extreme heat, the egg becomes hardened. This hardening is akin to letting the situation make you callus, pessimistic, and stubborn. Again, the circumstances win. Or are you the ground coffee beans? This ingredient had the same amount of heat as the other two. The difference was the coffee grounds used the challenge to create a new environment—the robust flavor of a perfect cup of coffee. Don't be the potato whose resolve was crushed by the circumstance. Don't be the egg who gets beaten up by life and becomes skeptical and unrelenting. Be the ground coffee beans that accept the situation for what it is and chooses to use it as an advantage, thereby changing its environment into something more appealing.

EXPERIENCE

"Young man, what makes you think you can provide for these two young girls?" Those were the words from a Texas judge as I stood before her making the case to voluntarily obtain full legal custody of my two younger sisters. As a twenty-two-year-old at The University of Texas (🤘 Hook 'em!), I went from college student to father figure overnight. My sisters were twelve and fifteen years old at the time. I won't bore you with the poverty porn. I will give you the reason I decided to alter my life and theirs. I told the judge, "I can at least give them a meal every night." At the bang of her gavel, I opened myself up to a world of challenges unbeknownst to many twenty-two-year-old college students. That day in May of 1998 changed my life for the rest of my life. I had peers tell me they couldn't have done what I did. I didn't understand it. Why wouldn't you? Why couldn't you? What made me so special? No disrespect to any of them. Several went on to be very successful—more successful than me. This pressure just so happened to be *my* privilege, not theirs.

I learned quickly that $8.80/hour as a bank teller wasn't going to be enough to cover the expenses that came with twelve- and fifteen-year-old girls. I was so stupid. My thinking was way off compared to what they actually needed. *Had they been boys,* I thought, *it would have been as easy as making sure they had a fresh pair of kicks and their fade was tight and everything would be good.* Not the case here. Because they were girls, I wanted to make extra certain they felt secure, looked nice, and were well taken care of. I also needed to develop the motherly ability to nurture their emotions through this transition. Yeah right! Where was I gonna get that from? Didn't matter. *Make it happen* was all I kept telling myself. This in addition to finding new accommodations for the three of us (sharing a two-bedroom apartment with my fraternity brother was no longer an option) and keeping my word of making sure they always had a meal became my primary goal. At my current hourly rate, that math didn't compute. I sought other positions at the bank, but limited experience and the lack of a degree made moving up a no-go. Every time I inquired, I felt like the rabbit in the cereal commercial. "Aww, silly rabbit, Trix are for kids." Another way of saying, "Silly bank teller with no degree, you're not qualified." My next move was to go to my financial aid officer on campus to see what solutions they had. I was blessed enough to qualify for additional grants due to my situation, but it still wasn't enough. After several trips to his office, he became something like my professional campus dope man employed by the university. I had a dire need (lack of money). He had temporary escape from reality (loans) that came with a cost (debt). The ends justified the means. I was in that Malcom X *"By any means necessary"* mode as long as it meant I could provide a better life for my sisters. I didn't care about the delayed ramifications it would have on me. They came first.

Like an addict that has an epiphany on their way to get that next high, I remember having a thought that hit me like my mom's backhand smacks to the face. 🥴 💬 *Rod, you know you're going into debt, right?* I cut my trip to the financial aid office short and detoured to the campus career services center. I went to the first adult I could find that worked there and asked for help getting a job. I needed what I called, at the time, grown-up money. An hourly position wasn't going to get it for us. I needed a salary—a guaranteed paycheck that would put a roof over our heads, food in our mouths, and clothes on our back. This type of position would require much of my time. I could only have two. That meant something had to give.

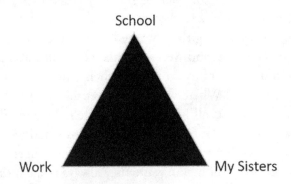

I couldn't do without working. How else would we eat? It couldn't be my sisters. I told a Texas judge I would take care of them, plus they needed me. Easy choice for me. I decided to forego the rest of my college education and enter the workforce.

Just because I had done something noble did not induce attractive offers from reputable industry-leading companies. C'mon now. This ain't that kind of story. All I had working for me was a compelling reason, but that wasn't a job requirement. I mentioned the tale of the tape before. If you've ever watched boxing or MMA, you're familiar with the phrase. If not, it's an expression usually used in sports to compare opposing participants in a game. It derived from boxing when fighters were measured using…wait for it…measuring tape. This isn't boxing, but make no mistake about it, the corporate game is just that—a game. You're always going to have an opponent. And yes, you will be measured against them. Announcers in boxing use the tale of the tape to assess the fighter's statistical chances for winning. One thing the tape can't measure is heart. And that's all I had. I just needed someone to give me a shot at the title. Not many wanted to. Would you after seeing this?

Not too impressive, I know. This is how I measured to everyone else who was vying for the same positions that I saw as the opportunity to put my sisters in a better situation. To my competition, it was all about getting a cushy job right out of college and securing a salary for bragging rights. For me it was about survival. Despite my need, I became more familiar with rejection than I did with advancing in the interview process. Thank God for placing the right people in my path at the right time to tell me just what I needed to hear.

One afternoon at a campus job fair, I met a gentleman from a leading bank in the industry. I felt I had an advantage in this arena since I had been a bank teller. Sure, the bank I worked for didn't see that I had the credentials to take the next step on their career path. Maybe this one would. In polished career fair form, I approached him with résumé in hand. I shook his hand, introduced myself, and began to sell my abilities. After giving him my textbook elevator speech, he had a conversation with me that would change how I played the corporate game for the remainder of my professional career. He gave me insight that the career services center on my flagship campus never revealed to me. His wisdom was so profound I couldn't understand why, out of all the books I was forced to read in school, I never ran across these words in any textbook. I couldn't understand why I had never sat in a lecture class where the professor uttered these words. He started by asking me, "What else have you done that's not on here? Employers want to see something that makes them say wow. Tell me, what have you done during your college career that would really impress me?" Now this wasn't earth-shattering at all. A basic question that I should have been prepared for. Oh, but he knew what he was doing—just softening me up for the knockout blow. What was he really asking for? Say it with me. My B side.

Shrugging my shoulders, I hesitantly, nearly ashamedly, mentioned the decision I had just made to take full legal custody of my two younger sisters. After all, why would that matter? I'm wasn't there to beg for grocery money. I didn't want a pat on the back or a pity party for the situation I voluntarily put myself in. I needed a job. He saw in that challenge something I was overlooking. He saw a narrative that needed to be told. He responded with, and this is what floored me, "You need to find a way to get that on this [pointing to my résumé]." He continued, "Are you on financial aid?" To which I answered, yes. At this point I was wondering was he trying to embarrass me or help me. He went on to say, "The other thing that needs to go on here is 'Responsible for 100 percent of my educational expenses.' That along with the decision you've just made shows a level of responsibility, maturity, sacrifice (which elicits an ability to work well in teams). Most of these kids in here don't understand what you've experienced, and an employer would see that as qualities they don't have time to teach. You have an advantage that most will never have." How perfect of an ending would it have been to say he hired me, right? Nope. I told you already, this ain't no fairytale. Instead he gave me a handshake goodbye and a "Wish you the best." I considered that interaction worth more than any salary I could have gotten. As a matter of fact, that conversation has been the reason I've been blessed enough to have some of the prestigious positions I've held in my professional lifetime. The Bible don't lie...wisdom is always worth more than riches.

I did exactly what he suggested. I had my résumé reflect that I was financially responsible for my education. I practiced how I would infuse my decision to assume guardianship of my sisters into my elevator pitch. I paralleled traits that employers look for with my decision and highlighted how that would not only translate into the workplace but also how no one else they interviewed would be able to compare to what I was bringing to the table. How did I handle the most glaring tale on the tape? Glad you asked. I was transparent and never gave the impression that I completed my college education. I didn't want to misrepresent myself. I did, however, downplay not earning my degree by ensuring that I know how I learn, which means I can learn anything if given the opportunity. My first win using this tactic landed me a job as an IT recruiter. Much like Belize, I had very little understanding of the IT industry, so I had to do a lot of internet searching. The jargon, the landscape, the intricacies were all foreign to me. So what! Like I said, for me it was all about survival. Next thing you know, I'm signing my first offer letter. The job in a reputable industry, the comfortable salary, and the ability to financially take care of my sisters was a reality.

That's when I became a believer that just because I didn't have the letters behind my name or the prestigious title of UT alumni didn't mean I was at a disadvantage. It did mean that I would have to work twice as hard as my degreed counterparts. No problem. I knew what I was signing up for when I made my decision. I felt as long as my compelling reason was the fuel for my actions, I had a chance. Let's get it and may the best person win. I had other positions after that one that gave me an opportunity to perfect and fine-tune my game. I became so confident in the process that I found myself ignoring job postings that said a degree was required. My thinking was, if I can get an interview, it's a wrap. Classic "Put me in coach" mentality. What I originally accepted as an immense amount of pressure in taking custody of my sisters turned out to be the privilege I needed to compete in the workforce. No one else I was up against had my story. When you realize you have something that others don't, that's privilege.

Let me be perfectly clear. I *am not* anti-education. People I know and don't know sacrificed for me to be able to get an education. I value what I was able to gain from my time on campus. I'm proud of the time I spent in college, and at times, I wished I had completed my degree. I'm in no way minimizing the importance higher education. If you can go to college, by all means, do it! Take full advantage of the resources and experiences college will provide. Despite not having a degree, I count myself as having learned a great deal in every class I took at the University of Texas. I may not be degreed, but I'm very educated. By no means am I saying you don't need a college degree. Remember, I just mentioned how not having a degree meant I had to work twice as hard.

The reason I feel comfortable sharing these secrets with you is because I'm counting on few, if any of you, being under the same circumstances that I had. Odds are you won't have to take custody of your siblings while in college. Chances are that you will graduate and get your college degree. That puts you at more of an advantage than me when I started on this corporate journey—and that's great! You've just magnified the output of everything you're learning here. Think of the results you'll have. Mine will pale in comparison. That's what I want! I want you to take my experience and the wisdom of others and excel far beyond the bar I've set. On the other hand, for those select few that find themselves in a similar battle, now you have hope. If it worked for me, it will work for you too.

Regardless of the situation, here's what I can guarantee. When you can leverage a challenge in your life and extract the principles, you give yourself a competitive advantage over your opponent. Pressure does just as much good as it does bad. As the saying goes, it can burst pipes or it can make diamonds. The privilege comes from knowing that everyone isn't able. Only the chosen, only the distinguished, only the select are adorned with pressure. It's a mantle that signifies triumph in the most uncomfortable circumstances. It's a reminder that only you could have overcome the obstacle you conquered. Only you could pass the test you were given. Only you would refuse to submit to the giant you took down. So continue to welcome the obstacle. Remind yourself of the test you passed. The same principle you used to slay one giant is the same principle you use to slay the next one. Go get what's yours. Understand that others couldn't handle your pressure; that's why it's your privilege.

WISDOM

When it comes to pressure, not everyone can handle it. Sometimes the moment is too big. Share how you've leveraged previous life challenges to give yourself a competitive advantage in the workplace.

When gold is refined (purified) by fire, it must go through a process to remove the impurities. Until then, it still contains traces of copper, zinc, iron, and silver. To remove these imperfections, the gold is heated in a furnace that produces heat up to 2,000° Fahrenheit. As the gold is heated, all the impurities rise to the top and are removed. Imagine the starch that rises to the top of a pot of rice as it boils— same thing.

I'm sitting in church one day when the minister uses the purification process to illustrate his point of the challenges people go through and why they go through them. He presents the story somewhat in the form of a riddle. He asked, "How many times must the gold be heated and reheated before it's finally pure?" In typical spiritual fashion, a smattering of biblical numbers fills the air: "Three!" I guess they got that from the Holy Trinity. "Seven!" Ah, the number of perfection, right? "Twelve!" You knew someone would say that one. The whole "Jesus having twelve disciples" thing. Wrong, nope, and…really? After everyone realizes that their answer is laughably incorrect, a hush comes over the crowd. With bated breath everyone awaits the answer. Then the minister hits us with "The gold continues to go through this process not three times, not seven, no, not twelve. The gold will continue to go through this uncomfortable process of being heated and reheated…until it cooperates." Making the point that we, too, will continue to be put in pressure situations not once, not three times, not seven, and no, not twelve, but as many times as it takes. We will continue to be placed in uncomfortable predicaments where we're tested, purified, pressured, and/or pushed to our breaking point…until we succumb to the lesson being taught and prove to be free of any impurities. Courtney Elveston mentioned this very example when we talked about pressure. Her advice: change your perspective when faced with pressure situations and ask yourself, How can this make me better? What good can I find in this that will help me grow? She wasn't alone. Others felt the same way.

As for life experiences that serve as leverage for getting through an intense moment, Joseph Norman has a reputation for having grace under fire. In his line of work, he has to. When I asked him what he draws on to get him through a jungle of irate customers, he told me his linchpin is his upbringing as a child. Growing up in the inner city where he had to figure out ways to handle adult situations as a child forged the person he is today. His thinking then, which is a principle for him today, was "I couldn't get shook and I couldn't lose it because I had to get out of there and make it happen." The same tactic works for him in his corporate setting. His approach to pressure parallels his approach to escaping a dysfunctional home: "Mom's trippin', Dad on drugs. The hood is dangerous. So what? Make it happen." It's the "so what?" part that should be magnified. To Joseph, everyone faces pressure. He says they might not demonstrate it outwardly but it's there. The "so what" simply means to him to "make it happen." This phrase came up when I was talking to Stephen Linton.

Stephen, like Joseph, also uses the extreme circumstances he had to deal with as a child to navigate pressure situations at work. For a young person that had to take care of himself for weeks on end while his mother wasn't around, he had no choice but to make it happen. Bills still had to get paid, he had to eat, and performing well academically was a must. He told me survival was his only option, which left no room for failing. "For me, it was fight or flight at all times. But where would I fly to because I had no options? So if you're not used to failing because it's never been an option, then you only have one option. You have to make it happen." It's this approach that he attributes to his success in the workplace.

Let's face it. Not everyone chooses to call on a challenging childhood for right-now motivation. That brings me to my conversation with Charles Epps. There was a certain work situation that pushed him to his limit. He wasn't having the success in this one area, and that was unusual for him. He was tasked with managing a safety program that would reduce the number of work-related incidents. After two years of increases in these types of incidents, he considered this to be a function that he didn't need to have responsibility for and concluded that it just wasn't a skill set that was in his wheelhouse. Once again, leaning on the wisdom of his manager, he learned that he should try putting extra focus on areas he may not have been paying attention to. Carrying out that simple directive gave him the confidence to have a different disposition when faced with a challenge. They put a bow on that project and moved on. The next obstacle dealt with software and the solution required someone that could code. This was an area he had no previous knowledge in, but he remembered the advice his manager gave him. In six months, Charles learned to code, and five years after he's been gone, the company is still using code that he wrote to manage the facilities. Charles forces himself to look at a problems or situations from a different perspective. This gives him the advantage he needs. "I open up my mind to possibilities that I didn't think about before and allow them to lead me in the right direction." Because he makes this a common practice, he ends up exposing himself to a variance of situations and has full confidence in his ability to solve the problem.

Here's a three-step process for making this happen for you the next time you encounter a pressure moment, complements of Steven Coleman.

1. Determine your well-formed outcome—what does the end result need to look like?
2. Figure out what previous experience(s) you've had that were similar to what you're currently facing.
3. Identify the resources you had at your disposal and how you used them—in other words what do you have attached to this situation that can help you achieve your outcome?

Regarding his second step in the process, he debunked the myth that the older you are, the more experiences you have in your arsenal. Not the case. According to Steven, "Even a twenty-year-old has enough pressure situations in their life to recall. They just don't know how far to go back." The human brain is much more sophisticated than we allow it to be. Scientifically, we have the ability to recall memories from about age three, proving that even for a young person in the workplace, surely there's at least one pressure moment they can recall in order to jumpstart this process. Maybe it's a Little League memory when you hit the game-winning shot. What about the time you broke your Mom's vase and came up with a clever way to disguise your mishap? Albeit devious, but the point remains that you found a way out of that pressure moment. You may not be able to relate to every detail in these nuggets of wisdom, but I implore you to grasp the transferrable principles they shared. Like Joseph and Stephen, you can leverage a challenging past to overcome a present-day problem. Like Charles, you may have to learn something different in order to come up with a solution. Thanks to Steven, you have a three-step process that's been proven to get results. One thing's for certain, if it worked for them, it will work for you. Wisdom like this is how you mitigate a lengthy purification process.

FACT

Remember the silly dares we used to throw at one another when we were younger? I bet you won't jump off the roof. I bet you won't kiss that girl. I bet you won't put your tongue on that frozen pole. Shout out to my man Flick from the movie *A Christmas Story*. What were we doing? We were offering up a pressure moment to reveal that hidden sense of value (in most cases stupidity) we wanted to see in ourselves or in others. In the Bible, David's purpose was to become king. Without Goliath that doesn't happen. There had to be a time of challenge in order to awaken the man he was destined to become. The best way to get David to come play was to tell him Goliath was on the playground. You're no exception. The best way to get you on the playground of your destiny moment is to thrust you into a situation that demands you to show up and perform despite the discomfort. A situation where the lights are on, the curtains are drawn, and the audience is waiting to be dazzled. Enter stage left, the antagonist named Pressure.

Everyone is aware of how diamonds are made. Squeeze a lump of coal together hard enough and out pops a flawless (FL) diamond. You don't have to be a connoisseur to know how wine is made. Step on some grapes then let the juice sit for a long time and eventually you get Screaming Eagle Cabernet Sauvignon 1992. My favorite is how the most impressive weapons of our time were made. Dip some iron in a bowl of lava, bang on it with a hammer, wash-rinse-repeat that forever, and presto, the heralded eighteenth-century Boateng Saber. Fact: some of the most extraordinary things ever made were created out of extreme circumstances. The same holds true for the birth of a child. Only a mother knows (so I won't even attempt to articulate) the amount of pressure it takes to bring forth a human being from her womb.

Let's talk about the FL diamond. Its purpose is to provide beauty and awe and brilliance that can be admired. When placed on a ring, it's meant to commemorate a momentous occasion. When placed on a necklace, it's supposed to captivate the room with its elegance. Diamonds have a purpose well beyond what I've mentioned.

However, without the pressure the diamond goes through, that purpose is aborted. We see the same principle with wine. A WebMD article suggests that there were several reports in the year 2000 that confirmed that wine (in moderation) reduces the risk of cardiovascular disease and heart attacks. We can then make the case that wine has a medical purpose. Google the phrase "uses for wine" and you'll find twenty unusual uses, twenty-nine novel uses, and twenty-seven genius ways. Here a use, there a use, everywhere a use-use.

Much like the diamond, without the pressure placed on the grapes, none of those uses are recognized. Probably the most important use of wine is sending you to your happy place after a long day's work. I'm certain that purpose would be missed the most. The same can be said for the making of a sword. Its purpose is to serve as a weapon. Absent the laborious process of forging the steel, and we'd still be using sticks and stones to break bones. Dr. Martin Luther King Jr. reminds us that "The ultimate measure of a man is not where he stands in moments of comfort and convenience, but where he stands at times of challenge and controversy." Said a different way, pressure exposes who you really are. Fact: there's greatness inside each one of us. You know it to be true, otherwise you wouldn't be reading this book trying to learn how to find that hidden treasure inside of you.

Sadly, not everyone will find their treasure. Every piece of coal will not become a diamond if it never experiences the pressure. Every grape won't get the distinction of becoming wine because some grapes won't experience the pressure. Every piece of metal won't be molded into a fine work of art without the pressure of the smith. But look at what pressure does. It uncovers hidden value. The FL diamond is privileged compared to the other pieces of coal. It went through the pressure and found its way onto a showroom floor. The most expensive bottle of wine in the world is privileged compared to all the other grapes. The process of pressing and fermentation brings forth a finish in the back of the mouth and throat unmatched by your typical produce-section grape. The most magnificent weapon ever created is privileged compared to a paper clip, staple, or any other everyday ho-hum piece of metal. The pressure of forging and the strength of the smith has shaped it with magnificence fit to demand seven figures on the auction block. Much like the diamond, the wine, and the sword, your true value would remain hidden without the trial of pressure. The privilege is in the finished product. Only after succumbing to the pressure will you ascend to heights reserved for a select few. Only then will you be able to lift your hands in victory while those that shunned the dust of the arena applaud your efforts. No longer is privilege reserved for those with favorable birthrights. The challenge that created the pressure process has given you privilege. Consider the playing field leveled.

Final fact: we all like feeling special. Look at pressure as if it were a private club with a selective intake process. You can't buy your way into this group. You can't sweet talk yourself into a membership. No amount of participation medals will get you past the door. In this club, social economic status and net worth mean jack squat. There's only one way to be counted as part of this elite group of individuals. It comes in the form of a question. What has pressure produced in your life? If it can't measure up to the diamond, the wine, or the fine craftsmanship of a sword, you're not getting in. To be counted in this group, you must have a story that rivals David's triumph. Show me your Goliath's head. What have you overcome? Give me an example of who you really are when tested by circumstances that only someone with Herculean shoulders can bear. That's your leverage. When was that moment for you? I challenge you to find it. When you do, you'll finally see how you've had an advantage all along.

The key is to search within you for that life experience that squeezed you, pressed you, and forged you into becoming someone privileged enough to join this exclusive club. You are the diamond because the pressure has given you purpose. You are the wine because being stepped on has released the greatness in you. You are the sword because extreme circumstances have made you a better version of yourself. Welcome to the club. The password is "Pressure is privilege."

CHAPTER 7

The Humble Narcissist

"Now I know what the void is...I'm a wire walker.
The void is my domain."
—Joseph Gordon-Levitt as Philippe
Petit in *The Walk* (2015)

On August 7, 1974 at 7:05 AM EST, a "once in a lifetime" event took place 1,350 ft. above street level between the Twin Towers of the World Trade Center. That was the day the people of New York saw a man walk back and forth from the North Tower to the South Tower (four times) on a wire suspended between the two buildings. One of the police officers positioned on the rooftop of one of the towers was quoted saying, "I personally figured I was watching something that somebody else would never see again in the world." For fifty minutes one of the most graceful performances and boldest acts of courage (along with a skosh of insanity) stopped people in their tracks with eyes intently focused on this one man. He not only made his way from one tower to the other four times but he also would occasionally burst into random theatrics in the middle of the wire between the two buildings. He stopped to take a seat... on the wire. He danced...on the wire. He laid down to rest...ON THE WIRE! His name is Philippe Petit. He's an accomplished aerialist, juggler, and unicycle rider. Six years prior to the erection of the iconic buildings, he imagined himself suspended in the balance between the two structures. Why? Petit's answer was simple, "I see three oranges, I have to juggle. I see two towers, and I have to walk." That day on the wire was the best example of what we'll discuss in this chapter.

We're going to dive into the skill it takes to walk the fine line between humility and confidence and self-promotion and promoting others. Both are necessary in the business world. Too much of one or the other and you'll fall off the wire. Thriving in professional setting requires that you make your presence and value known in whatever space you're functioning in. After all, who lights a lamp and puts it under a basket? For that light to serve its purpose, it's placed on a stand and it gives light to all in the house. In an ever-so-subtle way, you almost need to hit 'em with the Liam Neeson line from *Taken*, "But what I do have are a very particular set of skills—skills I have acquired over a very long career." You gotta let 'em know, right? That's the necessary aspect of self-promotion. Be careful though. Too much of it can be detrimental. You've seen it. It's the person that feels a need to read you their résumé at any given opportunity. All you wanted to do was introduce yourself with a handshake and say hello. Next thing you know, they've given you their work history, educational background, key accomplishments, and their hobbies. A person like this is typically all about themselves and is soon ostracized or, worse, tolerated out of obligation. No one should want to be that person.

The extreme alternative then is shining the light on others and retreating to the background where your skill set is camouflaged in the landscape of your peers. Sure, you can hope that someone stands in the gap for you and endorses your abilities. But why leave that to chance? That's something you should have control of. This is your career, your livelihood. Based on this theory, you'd be putting the outcome of your professional advancement in the hands of others and hoping they acted in your favor and at your pace. C'mon now, you know that ain't hap'nen. Then what do you do? Constantly going around flying a figurative banner that reads "LOOK AT ME!" will work against you more than it will for you. On the other hand, muting your attributes and hoping they're seen by the right person at the right time will work eventually, but like I said, you should be the one driving that train. Add to the equation that I've already told you in a previous chapter to let the spotlight find you, and you've got yourself a nice ball of confusion. What do you do? Should you self-promote and risk coming off like a pompous jerk, or do you let your skills do the talking and hope the right person is listening? Adopt the approach of our famed wire walker, Philippe Petit, and operate in the void.

The void is that space between the two points of reference. It's where the balancing act that takes place. The void is where you find the wire that connects humility and narcissism, cocky and confident, the mild-mannered and the show-off. Choosing to be more of one than the other is equivalent to a wire walker leaning completely to one side of the line. The only result you're getting with that strategy is falling off the wire all together. The audience came to see you operate in the void. They came to see you give a performance in the middle of the wire, the wire that connects the *necessary* and the *evil*, proving that you can be just the right combination of the two extremes. This is your domain. This is where you need to live.

EXPERIENCE

I remember the time I had two complete strangers give me two completely different assessments of my personality within a matter of thirty-six minutes—no joke, I timed it. It was during a culture transformation workshop at the company I worked for at the time. There we were in a room, forty of us. We were strategically invited to the training based on our business function. Everyone was part of the same line of business but operated in different capacities: sales, operations, underwriting, new business, claims—multiple factions within insurance. Most of us had never met many of the others save an e-mail exchange here or there. During one of the exercises, we were asked to pair up with someone we didn't know and complete an activity. Whatever we were asked to do had me recalling something that would happen to me when I spoke in small-group settings and how it made me feel. I remember sharing how I'd been in group meetings and introduced a concept or new idea, and afterward, no one had any questions for me. No one challenged me. No one asked any more of me than what I just gave. I would speak and there would be crickets afterward.

I work on practicing good communication skills anytime I have the stage, as anyone that frequents it should. But *surely*, I'm not that good to where no one would have any questions, comments, or concerns regarding the message I had delivered. I would purposefully leave out information to elicit a question. Radio silence. To make matters worse, I would find out later that once I left the room, the questions would begin swirling. As if I had never asked. It's like that scene in the movie *Friday* when Smokey says, "I got mind control over Deebo. When he say shut up—I be quiet. But when he leave, I be talking again." I've had another manager tell me that after I trained her group, as soon as I left the room, everyone started talking again. But while I was in the room, they had nothing to say. I guess I came off like Deebo and everyone in the room felt like Smokey. Not something I was proud of.

After explaining this to my workshop partner, she looked at me and said, "It's because you're too confident. You're intimidating. Hell, when I first saw you, I thought, *There's someone that has his $@&! together.* I mean look at how you dress, how you carry yourself. I was hesitant to interact with you the first time I saw you." Now, it would have been very easy to find the compliments in what she said, but all I could do was focus on the fact that I was leaning too much to the narcissistic side of the wire. As expected, I fell off and created an image of myself that I wasn't proud of. Immediately, my mood elevator hit the basement level. She hit me with a flurry of character traits that had me punch-drunk and down for the count.

Like any dazed fighter, I made a feeble attempt to get out of the corner and land some blows of my own just to save face. I responded, "But I purposefully *did not* come in here looking for the spotlight. I made it a point to lay low so no one would think I was trying to be that guy. I deliberately withheld a lot of comments during the day so I wouldn't be the dominant voice in the room."

She knew she had me though. Like a boxer that senses the knockout coming, she turned me right back into the corner and hit me with "You don't have to say anything. It's all over you." To her defense, she had no malicious intent in giving me this feedback. Her heart was in the right place and I trusted that. I knew she was being kind and honest. Plus, I had asked for it. She apologized profusely, but all I could do was think about the fact that I was unapproachable. How many others felt the same way and didn't say anything? It took me back to my middle school and high school days when we were broke and couldn't pay the water bill; I would have to go to school funky. No one wanted to be next to me. It was that all over again except this time the stench wasn't body odor. It was something called eau de parfum arrogánce. Saved by the bell—it was time for lunch. I retreated to my corner in deep thought as to how I could remove this Deebo-ness that was all on me. Others might bask in being the bully in the room, but that's not my game. You don't achieve Corporate Swagger by instilling fear. There are times when you need to draw the line in the sand and let people know, "Don't bring it here." Then there are times when you need to be as gentle as a dove to show you can be approachable and kindhearted.

Thirty-six minutes later—I told you I counted—I walked back into the main room from lunch and the facilitator stopped me. She said, "Rodney, I've been meaning to tell you, from the moment I saw you, I noticed you had such a charismatic way about you. It's gravitating. You carry yourself with such an aura that just made me want to know more about you—very inviting. From the way you dress to the way you speak, it's just very magnetic." She went on to comment about my mannerisms and how I had this mild-mannered quiet confidence that wasn't overpowering but definitely visible. I'm no FBI behavioral analyst, but to me, everything she said was unscripted and came from a genuinely sincere place. Amid her kind words, I was standing there looking like I was trying to solve one of the seven Millennium Problems. What just happened? Was this a joke? A little over a half hour ago, someone read me and concluded I was coming off like an unapproachable self-absorbed sunna-funna. Now I'm hearing how I have this gravitational pull that's clothed in a modest confidence. Neither of these people had ever set eyes on me prior to this workshop, and neither of them conspired to throw me into this state of confusion. In the end, I chose to believe both of them—they both spoke the truth. It was just coming from two different perspectives. The challenge quickly became how I appealed to both of them at the same time without losing who I was. The answer: better balance.

Therein was my opportunity to confront the void, mount the wire, and proceed to the middle to deliver my own theatrical performance, a performance that demonstrated my ability to be both mild-mannered and assured of my executive presence. How did I do it? The same way a skilled wire walker traverses a wire: with optimism, precision, and boldness.

Optimism—I had to remain positive and believe I could achieve a balance between the two assessments. I got rid of that defeated mentality that wanted me to think she was trying to "come at me, bro." I chose to think about the fact that I could dial it back to meet the expectation of my audience.

Precision—my actions had to be calculated. A wire walker knows how to walk, but doing it suspended in the air when the wrong twitch of a muscle can be life ~~altering~~ ending is different. What used to be automatic now requires a series of calculated movements. You can't simply do what comes naturally. In order to walk this line, you have to consider all the variables: what you say, how you say it, who you're saying it to, how they may take it. All this is done "in the Matrix." That's when it happens in real time but in super slow motion in your head. I decided to take a better inventory of my word choice. I purposefully crafted my sentences in a manner that couldn't be felt as condescending. I carefully inserted moments of self-deprecation to become one with my audience. I didn't want to seem too polished. I knew my presence would emit nodes of confidence, so mixing it with humility in my speech would make for the perfect balance.

Boldness—I had to deliver. When Philippe Petit hung his wire that summer morning, he created an expectation that he would walk it. The audience anticipated him leaving the safe confines of the platform and ultimately end up navigating the void. Until he did that, there was no show to see. There had to be a moment of boldness to put this whole thing into action. The same is true when attempting to display the ideal balance between two polar opposite character traits. I waited for my time to make resounding remarks. Short, concise, mic-drop-type statements that were fully inclusive of others. Rather than fashioning them in the first person only, I gave examples that included comments from others: "It's like Jake said…" I learned a valuable lesson on balance that day in the workshop. The way to approach the void is to use optimism, precision, and boldness. When these three are working in harmony with one another, it's just like Philippe said, "My left foot was on the wire, and my right foot and the weight of my body was anchored to the solidity of the tower. Without asking me, my right leg went on the wire, and there I was walking."

WISDOM

There's a fine line between humility and confidence. How do you walk that fine line without leaning too much to one side or the other?

I once heard a former CEO of a prominent company give a piece of advice on talk radio. She was asked to leave the listeners with a nugget of professional advice. Her response had such a rhythmic cadence to it that I repeated it over and over as if it were lyrics to a song. She said, "It's not who you know. It's not what you know. It's who knows what you know." Think about that for a moment. She was basically asserting that if left to stand on its own, your knowledge of all things academic and technical is not enough. Your connections gained from tireless hours of networking mixers is futile by itself. What paves the way for success in the business world is a combination of the two. Who knows what you know? You earn mad street cred (in a professional sense) when the right person/people are fully aware of your skills and capabilities. Her wisdom says that self-promotion is a skill you can't afford to ignore. I strongly suggest making sure to mix it with a balance of humility to avoid getting your face cracked.

Exhibit A. When I asked Alexandra this question, she was reminded of a fellow realtor she worked with. This person, she says, was constantly bragging on his numbers, how many houses he'd sold, and how much money he'd made. One day, he popped off at the mouth and said, "Don't you know who I am?" Outside of television, who actually has the audacity to ask that question to real people? He did. Being exhausted of the antics and wondering if there was any merit to his claims, Alexandra investigated. Side note, in this information and data-driven age we live in, everything is recorded somewhere, so don't fly too close to the sun, Icarus. Anyway, using means available to everyone in the company, Alexandra found that this person's production did not match the level of braggadocio he spewed. As she puts it, "I looked up his production and I'm kicking his @5$. I had to finally tell him, 'You know I can look up your production, right? So we're going to stop having this conversation of how much you've sold because we both know the truth.'" This was a classic case of someone leaning too far to the narcissistic side of the wire and falling off.

Sometimes it is necessary to exude a higher level of confidence, and it can be done strategically. Lesia Linton told me point-blank, "I have to be more narcissistic to make sure they know what I'm capable of doing." I'm not female, so I won't pontificate on something I'm biologically unqualified to explain. I will say that, as a minority, I agree that some work environments demand a more assertive stance. I found Lesia's comment to be echoed when I talked to Tyra Metoyer. I almost dropped the phone after I asked her how she balances humility and confidence. Before getting into her answer, she hit me with "First of all, the myth of meritocracy is crap!" Okay, not the way I thought it would start, but let's get into it. Tyra firmly believes there's a risk with being passive and letting your work speak for you. Sometimes merit alone isn't enough, so you have to take extra precautionary measures. Hers is a more intentional approach to combating partiality. She went on to say, "You might get overlooked, so you have to work hard. You have to be smarter. You have to have a lot of favor. You have to have the right relationships." The recognition of putting in all this work according to her experience is "We get invited to these spaces because we're smarter. That comes from there being something there that makes people think you deserve a seat at the table. There's an amount of confidence that comes with that." The confidence was palpable when I heard her tell me there's no issue she can't figure out. Being solution oriented is not just about SEO on a resume. She's proficient at it and works hard to make sure the right people know this about her. Like Lesia, she feels she can't afford to leave this to chance.

The same is still true—balance is key. When you have so much confidence weighing down one side of the scale, how do you bring it back to center? Tyra knows that what she has is a God-given gift. Because she knows where the gift came from, she stays closely connected to the Person that gave her the gift. While her confidence earns her a seat at the table, she takes that seat fully aware that there's a lot of smart people that didn't get invited. Her balancing act requires her to be ever mindful of the danger of having a false sense of it being her own intelligence that got her that seat. She openly submits to not having achieved anything by herself. When she takes that seat, she knows it because she's been blessed with the best mentors, managers, and role models. It's similar to what I learned from Darryl. "On your way up the hill, you can afford to toot your own horn. This is telling people why you should be there. Once you get to the top of the hill, it's about tooting other people's horn. This speaks to who helped you get there."

There's an inherent challenge that most people face when attempting to balance these two weights on their personality scale. Sometimes being too humble can work for you or against you. When I talked to Summer, she admitted that this is hard for her. Summer subscribes to the same school of thought as Stephen Linton, "If you're cold enough at what you do, you don't have to brag about it." The fact is you have to get *cold enough* first. Trust me, it's a hard line to walk, but it's required if you want to walk among giants. Summer learned this the hard way. Early in her career, she chose to lean more to the humble side of the wire. When I asked what happened, she told me, "I was at a company for so long just because I was comfortable playing second fiddle."

Even though she knows self-promotion is not her strong suit, being overly humble and hyping up others resulted in a self-imposed glass ceiling.

As we continued to talk about this, it was clear that even for someone who finds this part of Corporate Swagger to be difficult, it's still possible to manage these two opposites effectively. "When it comes to talking about myself, I'm bad at that. But when it comes to flexing what I know, I'm good there. That's how I sell myself to my clients," she says. Therein lies her balance. She displays confidence by deliberately making sure her clients know she's exceptionally knowledgeable and competent in her field. The humility is carried out by way of lack of self-promotion. She chooses to let her work speak for her. Thoma operates under the same rules. His philosophy is to focus on being humble, and letting other people play the role of his narcissistic side. He does this by purposefully creating situations where people are forced to witness what he knows. Remember, it's not who you know; it's not what you know; it's who knows what you know. This gives him a captive audience and a stage to display his knowledge. Because he's done the work of descending into the particulars, he's assured himself of functioning in a safe place. He knows there's nothing they can throw at him that he's not prepared for. Bottom line: you have to know your stuff.

What happens though, when your confidence is lauded by others? After all, you put in the work. You made sure they knew what you were capable of. Now, you're at the table and suddenly showered with recognition for getting there. How do you handle that? When I asked Steven Coleman this question, without hesitation he responded with one word: empowerment. He painted his picture using Clarence Avant, nicknamed the Godfather of Black Music, as the canvas. I won't go into the details of Avant's story, but simply put, he's the person behind some of the most iconic people in music, TV, film, and sports. To Steven's point, the way to balance the praise that's birthed from your confidence is to empower others. Trust in the law of reciprocity, karma, or reaping and sowing...they're all the same principle. He continued to explain that if you will empower others, you will, in turn, be empowered. When you create success in others, people will inevitably inquire as to where they learned the skills, who taught them the processes, and how they were able to handle certain situations. When they do, all fingers will point to you. This is how Steven operates in his field. He says, like Clarence, he wants to be the mind behind it all without being the face. His practice is when the praise comes, he deflects it right back on the person giving the accolades.

Person A: Who taught you how to close deals like that?
Person B: (answering) Steven Coleman.
Steven Coleman: (responding to Person B) My part was small. You're the one who made it happen. I wasn't the one sitting with the client. That was all your hard work that made that happen.

Even though some are shady enough not to do what's right, most people feel obligated to recognize those who helped them along their journey. Empower enough people, and the odds are in your favor that you'll be recognized. It wasn't until now that Avant's story has been given the attention it deserves. Until Netflix aired the documentary, you probably never heard of him—I hadn't. A lot of the people he's helped are way younger than him, which means they were in the limelight well before he had his golden moment. That never mattered to Clarence. He stayed true to empowering others and being appreciated behind the cameras. Ultimately, this type of humility earns respect, and you find yourself walking the line without a tremble in your step. Steven has based his entire business philosophy on it, and he continues to earn dividends.

One final food for thought on this comes courtesy of a meme that Charles Epps saw days prior to our conversation. The picture was of a maestro in front of an orchestra with arms raised in typical fashion while conducting. As he began to break down the meme for me, my classical music training kicked in and attempted to preempt the moral of the story with my own assumption as to where this was going. Even I didn't see this one coming. Charles explained that there are three things going on in the caption: there's an audience watching it unfold and enjoying the show; there's an orchestra that's responsible for executing the plan that's been laid out; finally, there's the director charged with leading the group and directing the flow. This person summons the extent of their expertise and talents undergirded by years of tutelage for the benefit of the former two groups. The caption to the meme read, "IF YOU WANT TO BE THE DIRECTOR, YOU'RE GOING TO HAVE TO TURN YOUR BACK ON THE CROWD." Yes, you need to advocate for yourself. Yes, it's necessary to make sure the right people are aware of your competencies. But if you want to be revered in the workplace and walk the fine line between narcissism and humility, the equation is clear. Do the work to show the audience you're deserving of standing on that platform center stage, and empower others to achieve their fullest potential. I like to say that being a humble narcissist is about carrying yourself like you know you're the &%@$ without smelling like it.

FACT

Too much exercise without rest can be harmful to the body. Too much work at the office without a break or vacation can create burnout. Too much discipline without freedom is enough to give a child a license to turn up when they leave for college. Some of you know exactly what I'm talking about. I digress. Fact: too much of anything is not good for you. When you're out of balance, something is going to suffer. One person can squat the weight of a mid-sized car. Impressive, but get at me in a few years when your knees are shredded and you can't walk a flight of stairs. Another person can't hold their own body weight. Not good either. What if you need to throw them paws (have to defend yourself—stay with me)? Balance is critical to every part of life. Professor Stan Lee taught us that when he introduced us to Thanos. All he wanted was balance. But you're not Thanos, and there are no infinity stones to collect in this movie.

I'm going to ask you to imagine you're an enthusiastic aerialist planning to walk across a 138-foot gap between the Twin Towers of the World Trade Center. I know it's probably not something you're aspiring to be, but just go with me. Let's say the North Tower represents a humble disposition and the South Tower, the temperament of a narcissist. The core reason for attempting such a harrowing act has something to do with ego and entertainment. That said, a show must happen so the audience can have an experience they'll talk about for years. This all starts with you. They came to see you elegantly glide across the wire in a way that makes them believe it's as effortless as breathing. This is no different from life in the business world. There's always an audience: coworkers, managers, executives, an interviewer. There's always a show being conducted: your presentation, your interview, your daily job function. There's always a desired outcome by the audience and, simultaneously, a desired impression you should always look to make. That outcome and desired impression is one that leaves them talking about you (in a favorable light) long after the performance has concluded. They're hoping to see you dazzle them with your ability to exceed their expectation in the workplace, and you want the same thing since your agenda is to gain credibility that you'll use as currency. One day you'll exchange that currency for a promotion, a new contract, or more responsibility—whatever moves your professional career forward.

Let's say you begin to get cold feet before stepping out onto the wire. You just stand there on the "humble" platform of the North Tower looking as if you're going to do it but never taking a step. All your time is spent firmly planted on the safety of being who you've always been—Jane/John Humble. You don't end up going anywhere because you're afraid to be anything but humble. It's too risky to embrace a different way of interacting with the audience. What if you fall flat on your face? After all, you are who you are and you shouldn't have to adjust your demeanor for anyone, right? For the sake of being comfortable and safe, you remain anchored on the North Tower of "humility," and no one ever sees a reason to give you any more credit than they already have. No credibility gained. No currency earned. There will probably be no subsequent exchange of professional advancement.

Successful leaders do possess a level of humility. When used at the most opportune moments, it does wonders for motivating others because it shines the light on their potential. Everyone likes the person that can admit their shortcomings and mistakes. Who doesn't want to be in the room with the person that gives appreciation and credit for the idea that becomes the catalyst for positive change in the organization? Fact: being humble causes people to like and respect you. But you say, "There you go, Rodney. See! I'm good staying on the North Tower. I want to be liked, and being humble sounds like the way to get people in my corner. I'll just stay here perched on this platform and not even worry about that wire."

To that thought I respond, in the words of Lee Corso, "Not so fast, my friend!" Remember, too much of anything is bad for you. That includes being humble. Although it's a virtue, if unbalanced, it will also carry with it disadvantages. If you're spending every opportunity touting someone else's accomplishments, you risk people questioning if you bring any value to the table. If Daphne is always getting the accolades, which in turn increases her value in the eyes of the group, why do we need you, Kenny? If your audience (your boss, peers, network, senior management) seldomly hears about your value or the ways in which you're driving positive change, they could very well wonder if you're doing anything significant at all. We've already learned that everything is an assessment. That being the case, the lifespan of your professional trajectory rests on making sure people know how important a role you play on the team and why they can't afford to let you go into free agency. Spend too much time being the soft-spoken people pleaser and decision-makers will doubt if you have what it takes to command a room.

We all know what happens to the player that gets buried at the end of the bench. Those are the best cheerleaders. They're good at lauding the efforts of the starting five. They never see the floor during meaningful game time. They made the team, so clearly, they have what it takes. Why are they on the bench? They've become so good at lifting others up that they're now seen as...well, let's just say there's a reason it's called garbage time—think about it.

That bring us to the South Tower, the narcissist. I've shared with you the fact that there's a danger that comes with staying on the North Tower. Being too humble can backfire, so be careful. You probably figure the easy thing to do is take the elevator down to the ground floor, walk over to the South Tower, take the elevator up to that platform and chill out there. ⊖ ⊘ ⬤ Don't do that either. Once again, I hear you. "But, Rodney, you said it's not who you know, it's not what you know, it's who knows what you know. So I need to let 'em know!" I also said that too much of anything is bad for you. Let's examine the facts from this vantage point.

This South Tower represents the hyperconfident person. This cat makes me laugh. Verbally, they admit being a learner, being coachable, and complying with other's assessment that they still have more to learn. They're convincing when it comes to their desire to self-develop and take feedback—even feedback that points to areas of improvement. Here's where they become comedy. Put a self-assessment in front of them that asks them to evaluate their skill level in any number of areas: emotional intelligence, communication, being a team player, anything. They'll grade themselves all fives (five being the highest) with no shame whatsoever and dare you to challenge them. This person is satisfied with the view from the South Tower.

They come dressed like a wire walker, but they don't have any intentions of leaving the narcissistic platform. They've operated from there for so long, and unfortunately, someone has rewarded them despite their behavior. Now they're justified to sit right there on the "narcissist" platform and never move. Fact: just as being humble makes people like you, once you're identified as a self-indulgent jerk, you'll push people away and short circuit your professional advancement. No one wants to be around the big-headed loudmouth who tells stories with one main character—themselves. Few will want to be teammates with the person that's always pointing to the name on the back of his/her jersey. Guaranteed this person will get in the driver's seat of a bus and run you over if it means they get to their destination before you.

Sure, letting people know your value and doing everything in your power to remain relevant is important to your professional growth. If you're trying to win that contract you *better* let them know how you get down—that no one will be able to do the work like you. Got an interview for a new role. That's your time to turn the spotlight on, make sure it's bright, and step smack-dab in the middle of that joint to let them know what you can do. I'm a firm believer in the rule we talked about earlier. It's who knows what you know. If you don't let them know, then you're left hoping someone else will. You shouldn't be willing to put such a responsibility of advancing your career solely in the hands of others. It's a good thing there's a wire that brings these two towers of thought together. The only answer is balance. Time to confront the void.

If being too humble can backfire and being a narcissist is a turn-off but both are necessary, that only leaves one option. You have to balance between the two. The answer is easy. The execution is where most people fall—pun intended. Staying with our wire walker analogy, I'll ask you this. What piece of equipment have you seen any tightrope or wire walker take with them into the void? That's right, a sandwich. Had to make sure I had your attention. No. You'll always see them with a balancing pole in hand. The purpose is in the name. Making the walk is hard enough. Without the balancing pole, it would be even more difficult. I wouldn't ask you to get out there and attempt to balance between being humble and narcissistic without giving you everything you need to make the walk a bit more feasible. You'll find your balancing pole in the next chapter.

To achieve true Corporate Swagger, like Petit, we must first see this as a performance that enthralls an audience and fills them with amazement. Next, it is essential to get over the doubt, silence the noise of the city, step out onto the wire, and confront the void. Finally, when both feet are suspended above the clouds and all that remains is you and the wire between humility and narcissism, use the tool in the next chapter to successfully give your audience the show they expect. When you understand the final component of Corporate Swagger, you'll find that everything you've learned will come naturally. Like Petit giving his audience a show they would never forget, you, too, will leave a memorable impression on your audience. They'll see you dance on the wire, take a seat on the wire while you enjoy the view, even allow the wire to serve as a place of rest. Your goal isn't to make it to the other side. No, the void is your domain. This is where you fully embrace the beauty of being a humble narcissist.

CHAPTER 8

First of All, Servants of All...

"With great power comes great responsibility."
—Uncle Ben,
Marvel comics character

Maybe this chapter should have come first. Had I done that, you may have been the only one to continue reading. Let me caution those of you considering tapping out, anticipating that you know what's coming and you're good with what you have. Remember, you don't have your balancing pole yet. You may have just enough to climb that ladder of success, achieve levels of notoriety, and earn a decent income. Failure to comply with this final requirement of Corporate Swagger will result in you leaving a path of destruction behind you. Approach the void without this in your hand, and well, you see where this metaphor is going. Let's just say it ain't go'n be pretty—literally and figuratively. Now that I have your attention, 🎶 🎵 "I shall...proceed...and continue...to rock the mic🎶 🎵." Shout out to The Roots for that line.

"Ils dovient envisage qu'une grande responsabilité est la suite inseparable d'un grand pouvoir." These were words found in a passage of decrees during the French Revolution at the 1793 French National Convention. The translation is "They must contemplate that a great responsibility is inseparable byproduct from a great power." In 1817, there was a debate in the United Kingdom House of Commons. One

139

of the members of the British Member of Parliament, William Lamb, spoke up and said, "The possession of great power necessarily implies great responsibility." In 1906, Winston Churchill said something similar, "Where there is great power there is great responsibility." His version is closely related to what we're more familiar with—the 1962 Marvel comic version spoken by Uncle Ben. While schooling Peter Parker on the obligation that comes with his newfound gift, he told him, "With great power comes great responsibility." What was Uncle Ben trying to tell the friendly neighborhood Spider Man? You see, the humble side of Peter Parker is an unassuming student that would prefer to run from the spotlight of attention. He's the nice fellow that sees a silver lining even in getting punked every day. He wouldn't raise a hand to hurt…a spider. See what I did there? On the flip side, he's also Spider Man. His confident side allows him to swing around town in a red-and-blue onesie. When he's in that suit doing what he was gifted to do, his self-esteem is on ten. There's no villain he can't beat. In stature alone, several of his enemies were bigger than him. Yet all of them fell victim to not his web but his heart for serving others. Could it be that William Lamb, Winston Churchill, and Uncle Ben are giving us the same message? Allow me to suggest that the meaning of the parable is also the tool needed to navigate the wire that connects humility and narcissism. Never approach the void without the balancing pole of service.

EXPERIENCE

When I made the move to working in the financial industry, I was adamant about making a name for myself. I didn't have a college degree or any other designations after my name, so I was in search for some type of educational validation. Going from being a music major to pursuing a career in finance was a big leap. My entire college curriculum was heavily weighted in all things concerning music and the fine arts. From my first day in class, my days were spent learning the structure of a French augmented sixth chord, learning how to sing songs in languages I couldn't speak, and making my piano professor's ears bleed. On paper I had no business even tip-toeing around the thought of becoming a financial professional. Primarily because I was broke. It's like being in fashion but having no sense of style. Again, none of that mattered—it was all about making it happen. Obtaining the same licenses that the typical Wall Street guy had would give me a feeling of acceptance. Those licenses would become my "degree," if you will. It didn't take me long to pass my exams and within a couple months, I was professionally licensed and legally equipped to practice in the areas of finance. However, the validation I sought was short-lived. Now I was just like everyone else in my field. I'd hear that snide voice in my head tell me, "So what! You got licenses, Rod. You're not special. Everyone in this industry has them. What are you going to *do* with them?" It was a you vs. you battle. No one ever physically uttered those words to me, but it was a constant fight in my own thoughts I had to overcome. There was truth in what that voice was telling me. Those licenses no longer set me apart. So I set my eyes on another form of validation—recognition.

One of the firms I was appointed with early in my career had an entrepreneurial business structure. I had to create my own book of business, set my own appointments, and close my own sales. My hunger for credibility in an industry that historically lacked a demographic that looked like me was what fueled my work ethic. That and food! A brother had to eat. Let's keep it 100. Yet still I craved not only a sense of belonging but also a strong desire to be recognized as a leader in this space. Winning in individual arenas was something that happened sparingly in my life. What was it like to be at the top of the mountain? How to you become the king of the hill? My view had always been from below, and I was tired of looking up at others.

Recognition was a big deal in this company. There was an award exclusively for newcomers. They called it the Pioneer Award. It was an award that was open to anyone in their first eighteen months with the company who ranked in the top 150 for life insurance production. We're talking about a global company with over two hundred thousand licensed agents and growing daily. Extract from that only the ones that are within their first eighteen month then carve out the top one hundred fifty. To make the Pioneer Award even more enticing, you were recognized at the annual convention that was held in the Georgia Dome—a freakin' professional football stadium! I'm not done. This conference is always packed. People come from all corners of the globe to applaud their peers for their accomplishments. The award ceremony for the Pioneer Award was a mirror image of a graduation processional. Oh, I'm not done yet. As a final touch to this spectacle, when your name was called and you proceeded to center stage to get your award, someone would shake your hand while another person would adorn you with a green jacket. No, not like the one Tiger, Phil, and Jack got for winning the masters but, yeah… like the one Tiger, Phil, and Jack got for winning the masters. Same shade of green, different emblem, but for a similar reason—to let everybody else know that you won. That was it! That's the mountain I wanted to climb. That was the environment I wanted it to happen in. Just like I cheered and clapped for others that got their green jacket, I wanted to have all those people applaud me as I walked across that stage. Bet! I knew what to do. I wasted my first six months in the company trying to figure things out. I had a year of eligibility left. Time to get it.

To make the Pioneer Club, you had to understand one thing: this was a marathon, not a sprint—18 months, 150 spots up for grabs, and thousands of people gunning for one of them. Starting the year with a good pace of closing cases and making sales was the easy part. Maintaining that pace for the entire duration was the real challenge. There was no set production number to hit. It was all a game of who has more. This was classic "big bank take li'l bank." In the span of a business day, you could see one person fall from the #1 to #10 spot depending on how much business they had go through the system the day before. The standings were that volatile. The one person you didn't want to be in the eleventh hour was the person occupying the 150th spot. That person could go to bed one night breathing a sigh of relief that they cracked the mark only to wake up the next day to see themselves fall out of contention.

With one hundred fifty people every year getting this award, you can imagine there are countless best practices and strategies that worked. It boiled down to two categories: individual producers and team producers. An individual producer is someone who wrote all the business themselves. Props to that person because they worked hard. The team producer benefitted not only from their own production but also from the production of the entire team. This person worked smart. Before you even say the word, if you have a job and you're not the CEO, then you're in a pyramid. If you're in management in your company or want to be in management, you, too, are/will benefit from the production of your team. My compensation was structured the same way in the manager role I had at AIG. At one time I had a team of twelve internal wholesalers. Every month, part of my compensation came as a result of the sales made in their regions. I wasn't selling, they were. But I got paid a small percentage of every sale that was made. My job was to get them to perform at their optimal level—for their benefit, the company's benefit, and mine. That's how business runs. As Mick Mulvaney said, "Get over it!" Now stop trippin' so I can make my point. Needless to say, I've always been a fan of the "work smart, not hard" option. Funny thing though, I didn't approach getting my green jacket that way.

When I got serious about being recognized as a Pioneer, I was nowhere on the radar of cracking the top 150. I had basically given everyone else in the company a six-month head start. Yeah, I know... procrastination. Like I'm the only one that does it. My production was so low compared to everyone else you had to hit Page Down on the keyboard several times before you saw my name. Honestly, I deserved to be at the bottom. I hadn't done the work. I refocused and got serious. I told my principal (the equivalent to a site manager or branch manager) what my goal was, and like any good mentor and coach, he told me, "You waited long enough to get started. It's going to be hard, but I believe you can do it." Little by little I began personally producing enough business to see myself move up the leaderboard. Nowhere near Pioneer status, but it was good to see the "ball go through the hoop," so to speak. Small victories like that helped my confidence and belief.

After a while, despite my individual efforts, I couldn't seem to make it over the hump. Like working out, I reached a plateau. I had gotten into the top two hundreds with about three months to go in the contest period. I remember whining to my principal about how hard it was going to be and how I was doing everything I could but I couldn't seem to get there. What he told me became the impetus for this chapter and the way I approach any goal—personal or professional. With a matter-of-fact tone he looked at me and grinned. That kind of grin a parent has when they see their child making the same mistake over and over. "That's your problem," he said. "You're focusing on yourself. Take the focus off you and help your team and you'll get there."

Immediately, it clicked. In that instant, I stopped thinking about me crossing the stage and began to imagine some of the people on my team reaching their goal. I needed to find out what motivated them. Until then I was clueless about what was important to them. Once I found out, I needed to give myself to their mission. For some reason, that visual became more attractive than the individual fantasy I scripted of walking across the stage and getting my green jacket. With little time left in the contest period and everything to gain, I immediately changed my course of action. I changed my mind-set to focus on my team. I changed my words by asking them what they wanted to accomplish. I changed my actions by pouring everything I had into helping them achieve their individual goal. I helped them with appointments, strategies, training, encouragement, whatever they needed. I didn't forget about the Pioneer Award. I stayed checking the leader board often. You know what? I got over the hump. Still hadn't cracked the top 150, but now I was so close I could smell it. You didn't have to hit Page Down on the keyboard to see my name anymore. When it was all said and done, I didn't end up making the Pioneer Club that year. By the end of the contest period, I would get no closer than #165.

I'm sorry. Did I set you up? I keep telling you, this ain't that kind of story. Even though I didn't make the cut, I learned one of the most valuable lessons in my adult life. Putting the focus on others helped me get higher. I know it sounds counterintuitive. When considering your ascent up the professional ladder, it seems as if there's no way subscribing to this way of thinking is conducive to upward mobility. That's flawed thinking, my friend. With that mind-set, you'll never experience sustained success. No, I didn't have my moment of fame.

However, I didn't experience defeat either. What I did experience was a feeling unmatched by anything I had ever felt. It's the feeling a parent has when they let go of the back of the bicycle seat. The feeling of seeing their child, who has fallen, finally riding by themselves. It was a transference of ability, confidence, and belief from me to the people on my team. It became less about me and more about seeing personal growth in others. I've used the same practice with every team I managed since then. Yes, like you, I have an agenda. I want to look good in the eyes of my peers, senior management, and clients. It's a harder game to play when it's all about you though. Take the pressure off yourself and use your talent, skills, and giftings for the benefit of the person coming behind you. That's your responsibility. Pour yourself into them and watch them summit higher levels of achievement. Your efforts in their life become the fingerprint that's seldom seen on the surface, but after further investigation, there's no denying you were there. You were a part of their narrative. Do it for enough people, and you'll become a legend in a sense. People will seek you out because of your track record. What you've really done is used your power in a responsible way. Uncle Ben would be proud of you too.

WISDOM

All good leaders are servants to some degree. How do you use this quality in the workplace or in business?

The responses were all the same, which tells me that it's not a secret. If you're missing this element in your game, your success will be short-lived. According to Darryl Blackburn, Vince Carter is the ultimate example of service and sustainable success. Drafted fifth overall in the 1998 NBA Draft, it didn't take long for Vince to become a household name with nicknames like Half Man, Half Amazing; Vinsanity; and Air Canada. Even someone that doesn't follow the sport can conclude that he must be a special talent. The display he put on in the 2000 All-Star Dunk Contest hadn't been seen since the likes of His Airness, Michael Jordan. Look up "Vince Carter Olympic Dunk," and you'll see a video of this 6'6" phenom leaping over a 7'2" grown man during a game in the Sydney Olympics—it was SICK! That was early in his career. His athleticism made him a productive piece for several teams in the beginning, but Father Time is undefeated.

After logging too many frequent flyer miles on those knees of his, Vince Carter had to find a different commodity to market to potential suitors. If he wanted to remain in the league, he had to convince NBA owners that he had a value, beyond the court, that couldn't be ignored. No disrespect at all to his game. At forty-two years of age, he could still fill it up; but let's be honest, college players are more athletic and have enough game to justify not signing Vince Carter. With the average NBA career being only 4.8 years, why is it that the 2019–2020 season will be his 22nd year in the league? As a result, he'll sit alone as the only player in NBA history to have such a tenured career. Darryl's answer, "His value is in his servitude. Teams are not hiring him because of his athleticism. His basketball skills have diminished compared to when he first got in the league, but his leadership skills have afforded him a spot on six NBA rosters in the past ten years. His commodity is his ability to teach the young players how to be a professional in the NBA." Therein lies the importance of service. To further drive this point home, I managed a *young* lady who had been with the company forty-two years. It wasn't her impeccable sales acumen that kept her employed. It was the wealth of knowledge she acquired during her tenure and the fact that she was a resource to everyone on the sales team—including managers. She's survived countless layoffs simply because there was literally no question, no situation that she didn't have the answer to or know who to call to get it. Her value was in her service to those coming in the door behind her. Looking for long-term success? Better come to terms with what everyone I talked to mentioned:

- Summer McElroy: "It has to be something more than money. Success comes from knowing you're doing good for other people."
- Courtney Elveston: "We rise by lifting others up. Sometimes that means getting in the trenches with them."

- Thoma Brewer: "Find a way to positively engage with others, and it will come back to you. The cutthroat mentality doesn't work. Always remember that someone had your back."
- Joseph Norman: "You *can* get high in the company not serving, but you won't have loyal advocates [minions] along the way. If you're serving people's best interest, you're creating loyalty. Now you have people you can reach out to if ever you're in a tight spot."
- Sarah Bolka: "It's the notion that, I exist to create a benefit to those around me. I want to give back more than what I take. Leaders eat last."
- Steven Coleman: "I'm trying to help the next person not be like me but be *better* than me. I don't want people I work with to make the same mistakes that I made. They should be able to do it better, faster, more efficiently—all because I chose to serve them."
- Veronica Brooks: "Service is the backbone of how I approach my job. Seeing opportunities to pour into others and help make them better lets me know I'm part of a team. When the team does well, I do well as a byproduct."
- Anthony Rosette: "I get 8K-10K steps in per day just chasing people down to get stuff done for people on my team. Ultimately, it comes back around because when a deadline can't be pushed back and we have to do extra work, I've earned currency to ask the team to work a little longer, push a bit harder to get things done."
- Byrena Washington: "The question is, who's your replacement? You should have instilled so much and taught so much that everything runs like a well oil machine when you're not there. That's the true power of leadership."
- Alexandra McCauley: "I give back by teaching. Teaching new agents reminds me of where I was five years ago and helps keeps me stay sharp on the fundamentals of having a successful real estate practice."

- Stephen Linton: "You'll peak at your success if you don't know how to give back. When you create successful people, it's going to always come back to you."
- Lesia Linton: "If you keep giving back, it makes you a better person. You learn something you didn't know when you volunteer to put yourself in a servant position."
- Charles Epps: "With everything you got, you should be imparting into someone else. If you have a full cup, you're at capacity and can't take any more in. This forces us to pour from our vessel into others. To simply walk around with a full cup is a waste. No one benefits but you."

I was already drinking the Kool-Aid, but the echo chamber of wisdom from this circle of influence was indisputable. If that doesn't do it for you, perhaps these final words from Tyra will wake you up. When I asked her this question, she broke it down into two parts: First, you have to understand that nothing is beneath you. Her suggestion is, in order to be a top performer, you have to let go of the mentality that claims doing _____ is not in your job description. Basically, if service isn't in your DNA, you probably need to redefine *work* all together. Second, and most importantly, we all stand on someone else's shoulders. That said, it's our duty to be the shoulders others can stand upon. "It's the rent we pay," she says. "As you go throughout your career learning and growing, your shoulders should be getting stronger." I'd imagine it's because the stronger you are, the more people you should be supporting. Tyra went on to say that if you don't have shoulders to stand on, then you're wasting space. For her, and everyone else that spoke to this subject, you don't serve others for what you can get out of it, but you always get something for serving others. This removes *title* from being synonymous with *leadership* and replaces it with *influence*. The mic dropped when she told me, "When you have influence by way of service, you don't have to worry about title and promotion, it will find you."

FACT

Studies conclude that when people have an opportunity to serve others in any capacity, they themselves experience a stronger sense of purpose and meaning in life. From that comes a better mental and physical well-being. To use another *Friends* reference, there's an episode where Joey tries to get Phoebe to understand that there is no such thing as a selfless good deed. The fact is, he was right. Get at me if you can find a good deed that doesn't make you feel good in return. You can't. Anytime you do something good for someone else, you usually walk away feeling good about yourself. It's called being human.

Ask a child what they want to be when they grow up, and you'll probably get the typical answers: fireman, doctor, a superhero. Who wouldn't want to be the person that everyone loves because of their amazing ability to rescue someone from a burning building? The surgeon can literally tout that he/she saves lives for a living. Albeit fictional, a superhero is someone known for extraordinary ability. I'll make it a bit more practical. Think of the allure that comes with saying, "I work in the tech industry." Imagine the attention you'd get when you roll into the networking event and let everyone know you're a lawyer. Put an insurance salesperson in the circle with those two, and you'll find out quickly which roles are sexy and which one isn't. All three professions are different in all but one way. They all share an element of service. Fact: we all want to serve. Some people just fight it longer than others. Eventually, we all give in to that yearning to give of ourselves for someone else's benefit.

Still not convinced? Consider if you will the culture shift happening in companies everywhere. Managers are being held to a servant-leadership standard. I was scrolling LinkedIn the other day, and I saw this depiction of two types of bosses. One frame had a person with a scowl on his face that was clearly the manager. He had one hand on his hip and the other pointing in a forward direction. Beneath him was another person, clearly the employee, in a subservient posture with a terrified look on his face. The caption above the manager was "Go!" The next frame had the same manager pointing in the same forward direction, but he had a more pleasant look on his face. Instead of placing the manager on a superior plane in the picture, he was positioned behind the employee. The facial expression on the employee's face was different as well. This time he was excited. He looked encouraged. The caption was the same: "Go!" Thus, the expectations in all work environments. Managers and people in leadership are expected to serve their team, attend to the needs of their employees, provide and create a welcoming atmosphere where employees can thrive. Illustrations like these are everywhere. It makes you check yourself if you're not on the right side of this spectrum. Are you forcing someone to serve your needs, or are you serving the needs of others?

Gone are the days when leadership was all about being disconnected from the people while perched in an ivory tower. No one wants to work for a manager that fails to provide the resources necessary to advance their career aspirations. One-on-one meetings with team members have become commonplace in roles of leadership. Employees know that you have a wealth of knowledge, otherwise you wouldn't be in that position. They long to sit at the feet of leadership and learn from those that have cracked the DaVinci code. They search for answers from the people who've already passed the test. They approach each day with the quiet hope that they'll bump into the person that will be willing to help them take the next step forward in their professional career.

As of this moment, the tables have turned. Your cup has been filled, and it's your obligation to pour into someone else. With the secrets that you've been exposed to, the playing field has been leveled. You've put in the time to learn a few new tricks. You've been armed with knowledge that can help you and that person coming behind you. You've been empowered to compete on a stage that statistically you're not qualified to be on—and win! Go get what's yours. But don't forget. With this power comes great responsibility.

My call to action is simple. Put what you've learned to use. First, hit me up on LinkedIn, Twitter, or Instagram and let me know how it's going. I want to know how you've put these eight concepts to use—the good, the bad, and the ugly. Hopefully there's more of the former than the latter two. Secondly, share your experience with someone who doesn't know the game. Serve others by leveling their playing field. If you do that, I promise that you'll always be on an upward trajectory personally and professionally.

It's time out for not competing because you think you don't measure up to the competition. It's time out for being overlooked. It's time that you show them you have value that can't be ignored. The secret is out. You now have a competitive advantage. Some call it the "X" factor. Others refer to it as having "it." Those that can't quite put their finger on it will say, "I don't know what it is, but there's something about you." It's because you've got your mind right, you look the part, you're multilingual, you own the stage, you have an interesting story; pressure doesn't bother you; you can walk the line between confidence and humility, and you have a heart to serve. Just tell them you found the secret to winning the corporate game. It's called Corporate Swagger.

About the Author

Born to a sixteen-year-old single mother on the South Side of Chicago, it was inevitable that struggle would be the cornerstone of Rodney's life and "underdog" his moniker. Growing up in a military household supplied a strong sense of discipline, causing Rodney to beat typical statistics for young men like him. With help from a loving set of choir teachers, Richard and Martha Surface, Rodney developed an affinity for the fine arts and was nurtured in the area of singing classical music. After graduating from Killeen High School, he went on to study vocal performance at the University of Texas. While in college, he voluntarily assumed full legal custody of his two younger sisters and made the decision to forego earning his college degree. This was the birth of what he now calls Corporate Swagger.

After experiencing a level of success in sales and management and spending two decades as a licensed financial professional, Rodney found his "why." With him, it's all about empowering the underdog to compete on a stage they're not statistically qualified to be on—and win! Whether it's speaking to large crowds, coaching one-on-one, mentoring with Big Brothers Big Sisters of America, traversing a Spartan obstacle course, singing in the Houston Symphony Chorus, or writing his first book, that's his only objective.

If there's anyone who can show you how to level the playing field, and more times than not, tilt it in your favor, it's Rodney S. Jones.